AF247590

MAN AND HIS RESOURCES

. . . In Today's World

MAN AND HIS RESOURCES

. . . In Today's World

by

C.W. Mattison

Formerly on the staff of the United States Forest Service and the New York State Conservation Department.

Joseph Alvarez

Published by

CREATIVE
EDUCATIONAL
SOCIETY, INC.

Mankato, Minnesota

MAN AND HIS RESOURCES

INTERNATIONAL COPYRIGHTS RESERVED IN ALL COUNTRIES

No part of this book may be reproduced in any form except for reviews, without permission in writing from the publisher.

Standard Book Number 87191-001-2

Library of Congress Catalog Card Number 66-25119

Printed in the United States

© COPYRIGHT 1967

by the

CREATIVE EDUCATIONAL SOCIETY, INC.

Mankato, Minnesota 56001

FOREWORD

by
Athelstan Spilhaus

*Chairman, National Academy
of Sciences Committee
on Pollution*

This book is about the marvelous resources for man's use and enjoyment in the land, air and waters on earth. But it warns against squandering or spoiling these resources. We dig from the ground iron ore that was concentrated by slow geological processes over millions of years but we throw away or allow to rust most of the metal that we make from it. We pollute our beautiful streams and lakes with wastes of civilization that poison them or fill them with green algae scum that make them not only useless but unpleasant by sight or smell. We pour smoke, toxic gases and smells into our atmosphere so that fresh air and life giving sunshine are blocked from the cities.

Science and technology can invent plastics and other synthetic materials to replace dwindling metals; science and technology can invent nuclear power plants to take the place of the fossil fuels — coal, oil and natural gas — when they become exhausted. But science and technology cannot invent substitutes for the natural beauty of the landscape, of the streams, lakes and the sea, or the kaleidoscope in the sky. The preservation of the aesthetic qualities of space on earth in which man can re-create his heritage of humanness is most important to every one of us. It can only be done if each of us recognizes the priceless environment we have inherited. Readers of this book will be helped to see their obligation to pass on, unspoiled, to future generations the living space on earth.

Contents

CHAPTER 1   THESE ARE OUR RESOURCES

CHAPTER 2   AIR

CHAPTER 3   WATER

CHAPTER 4   LAND AND SOIL

CHAPTER 5   FORESTS

CHAPTER 6   WILDLIFE

CHAPTER 7   MINERALS

CHAPTER 8   LOOKING TO THE FUTURE

Preface

RESOURCES: *Past, Present and Future*

The European settlers found the American continent a storehouse of natural wealth far beyond the imagination of the explorers seeking gold. It held a great variety of climate and growing conditions, of soils and vegetation, of waterways and land forms, and buried treasure in fresh water and minerals.

These bounties might have remained untapped had not the European pioneers and later generations used imagination, great effort, and resourcefulness to build farms, homes, highways, factories, and cities. An enterprising and industrious population multiplied and spread from coast to coast, converting the raw materials of the environment to clever uses. Along the way, to be sure, some of man's efforts were overambitious and led to the depletion of large quantities of natural resources. Personal greed, ambition, and public indifference caused forests to be laid waste, soil to be blown away, minerals to be overmined — and, more recently, air and water to be polluted. After a long struggle, the present generation is taking steps to make wiser use of the public heritage.

The battle is an ongoing one and needs the active attention and support of all people working through their lawmakers and government agencies. **Man and His Resources** presents the problems, the accomplishments, and the future outlook. There is much to be proud of — and much work yet to be done. President John F. Kennedy once warned that conservation will win when "each and every American makes the preservation of the beauty and bounty of the American earth his personal commitment." This book is presented to help fulfill that goal.

U.S. Forest Service

DuPont

CHAPTER 1

THESE ARE OUR RESOURCES

Conservation has been described as a state of harmony between man and the land. "Land," as used in this sense, includes everything on, under and above the earth — in short, all our natural resources. These include air, water, soil, forests, wildlife, and minerals.

Some of the resources — water, soil, forests, wildlife — are self-renewing when properly managed. Plants and animals reproduce themselves; forests and plant life thrive in soil that draws nourishment from sunlight, water, minerals, and plant and animal matter. Water falls to earth as rain, evaporates, rises into the atmosphere, condenses, and falls to earth again in a continuous cycle.

Renewable resources depend upon each other — and man depends upon them all. Forests cannot grow without water and soil; forests and grasslands help water to percolate into the ground; soil is kept in place by plant cover and enriched by plant and animal decay. The cycle has no beginning and, when operated in balance, it has no end.

Some natural resources are *non-renewable*. Coal, iron, oil, copper, and salt do not "grow" again. Once a mineral is mined, it cannot be replaced. Open space or open land is another non-renewable resource that is becoming a cause for concern. We are just beginning to realize how limited is this resource and how important it is to retain it, especially in crowded cities and metropolitan areas.

Other natural resources appear to be so limitless as to be inexhaustible. The sun, the air, and the sea are such resources. Only a small portion of the sun's energy, for example, is harnessed as power, but scientists are seeking new uses for solar energy. They are also seeking new ways of using the vast oceans as a source of water, food, and minerals. The elements in the atmosphere are a great storehouse for industrial needs. The potential of all of these resources is limitless; but misuse of them can limit their benefits, even destroy their usefulness.

Finally, there are the resources still to be explored and developed. Less than a century ago, workmen digging for salt discovered an oily substance which they discarded as useless because they were unable to separate the oil from the salt. The "useless" substance was crude oil, which is now one of our most valuable industrial products. Before 1940, uranium was a useless ore; today it is the source of atomic power. Who can tell what other resources will be discovered as man's numbers increase, together with his needs?

A Changing America

U.S. Forest Service

Colonists who came to America in the early 18th century found a land quite different from the one we know today. Lush forests covered the countryside and sparkling streams and clear rivers flowed through the hills and valleys. The air was pure and refreshing. Birds flew overhead, wild game roamed the woodlands and grasslands, and freshwater fish thrived in the streams and lakes. The land was silent, abundant, and beautiful.

The first settlers cut away the forests to build homes and clear the land for crops or they farmed the rocky hillsides. When the soil was exhausted, they had only to pack their belongings, conquer the rough trails over the Appalachian Mountains, and move into the fertile grasslands of the Midwest. The broad Mississippi River and its many branches served as inland waterways. Many of the adventurous and restless pioneers moved further westward across the continent, cultivating the soil, cutting the great forests, grazing the rangeland. Land itself seemed inexhaustible, as did its riches.

U.S. Forest Service

10

Then came the factories and their unquenchable thirst for fuel — coal, iron, copper, oil. Industry took hold and grew rapidly, devouring the supplies of oil, iron, trees, water, and even land. Immigrants poured in from Europe to settle across the continent; large numbers gravitated to industrial centers where work was plentiful. Smoke-filled cities and close-packed tenements e n c l o s e d them. Their only glimpse of nature was a green rim around the outskirts of the city or small parks inside.

Cities grew during those first 200 years of settlement, but it was still the farmers, miners, and loggers who worked the land to support the city dwellers. Forest fires followed logging and, without protection of plants, rich topsoil was washed away by pounding rains. Loose, overculti-vated soil was blown away by the wind. Some species of wildlife were hunted to extinction or their natural habitat destroyed. Then, as conditions became grave, the American people began to understand the need for practicing conservation.

Through legislation and the insistence of conservationists, many of our resources have been restored to usefulness. But problems remain. Now the focus is on streams and rivers polluted by chemical waste and sewage and on air that is choked with smog.

As our population grows in numbers and as the applications of science and technology make additional demands on our resources, we must find ways of working in harmony with nature instead of ruthlessly exploiting it.

How Natural Resources Affect Us

All living things depend upon the natural world for their existence. This is as true of man as it is of birds, fish, or gorillas. Our food, clothing, homes, automobiles, newspapers, books, furniture, heat, and electricity — all these are products of natural resources.

We lose sight of just how dependent we are upon nature. For example, the words you are reading are printed on paper. Paper was made from wood pulp which came from the trees of our forests. The trees grew on soil nourished by air, water, and sunlight. Soil, rock, and air were also used to produce the chemicals for the wood pulp. Minerals supplied materials with which to build and lubricate the printing presses. Even ink was made from natural substances. There is nothing we use that has not been derived in some way from natural resources.

Our mental health and happiness reflect the use made of natural resources. We need space for fresh air, privacy, and play. We need air, sunshine, trees, and grass to restore our energy and revive our spirits. If we are too long deprived of space, sunshine, trees, and flowers, we become tense, short-tempered, and restless. The bounty of nature in all

its forms — as a source of materials and as a source of beauty — is one of America's great assets and a source of concern. More attention is given today than in any time in our history to the use and management of land as cities spread to suburbs and suburbs into exurbia, and much of it engulfs the open spaces once needed for agriculture.

"We must maintain the chance for contact with beauty," President Lyndon Johnson said. "When that chance dies, a light dies in all of us. For over three centuries the beauty of America has sustained our spirit and enlarged our vision. We must act now to protect this heritage."

The Need For Conservation

Only man is able to shape nature to his will. This awesome power carries with it a grave responsibility to use nature's resources wisely. Our population is increasing and our industry is expanding. There is only so much land, water, soil, coal, iron and oil; and we must be sure that the demand for these resources does not exceed the supply.

Conservation s h o u l d not be thought of as avoiding the use of resources, but rather as *wise use and management* of them. Through conservation practices we can sustain and increase the supply for the future. The natural resources of the country are in the hands of the people. The manner in which they will be used will be no better than their understanding and beliefs.

Here are just a few of the problems that confront us. The United States has almost half a billion, 500,000,000 acres of cropland and almost an equal amount of pasture and range. Of the cropland, only 28 million acres, have no conservation problems and 136 million acres are properly managed. That leaves about 65 per cent, over 300 million acres, in need of conservation. In cropland, vast areas have been destroyed by erosion, excess water from inadequate drainage, unfavorable soil, and adverse climate. Almost 75 per cent of the cropland used as private pasture and rangeland needs conservation because of overgrazing, fire, erosion, rodents, brush, or inadequate plant cover.

As for forests, there are half a billion acres of commercial forest land, enough to grow the timber we need if good forestry practices are applied. But good forest management is used on only a small part of this land, which includes public forests and those owned by forest industries. On small, private forests good forestry is the exception rather than the rule.

About a fourth of the timber cut each year is wasted. Insects, disease, and fire kill 13 billion board feet of sawtimber each year — enough to supply the wood for a million homes! There are too few trees on 114 million acres of land, and the timber that is grown is declining in quality.

Many species of wildlife have been completely exterminated and others are in danger. Without protection and adequate habitat the populations of the American eagle, grizzly bear, California condor, whooping crane, prairie chicken, bighorn desert sheep, and polar bear will disappear.

The greatest danger, which has come to the forefront of public attention in the last two decades, is that of water and air pollution. This is a national, state, regional, local, and individual problem. To solve it will require billions of dollars, a great deal of research and legislation, and the cooperation of all sections of society.

It has become clear to all of us that the most important way to treat the conservation of natural resources is to view them as a whole. As we plan for one, we must also plan for the others. Man is part of the vast web of life, the balance of nature. If he does not conserve his resources, he will be the final victim of his own folly.

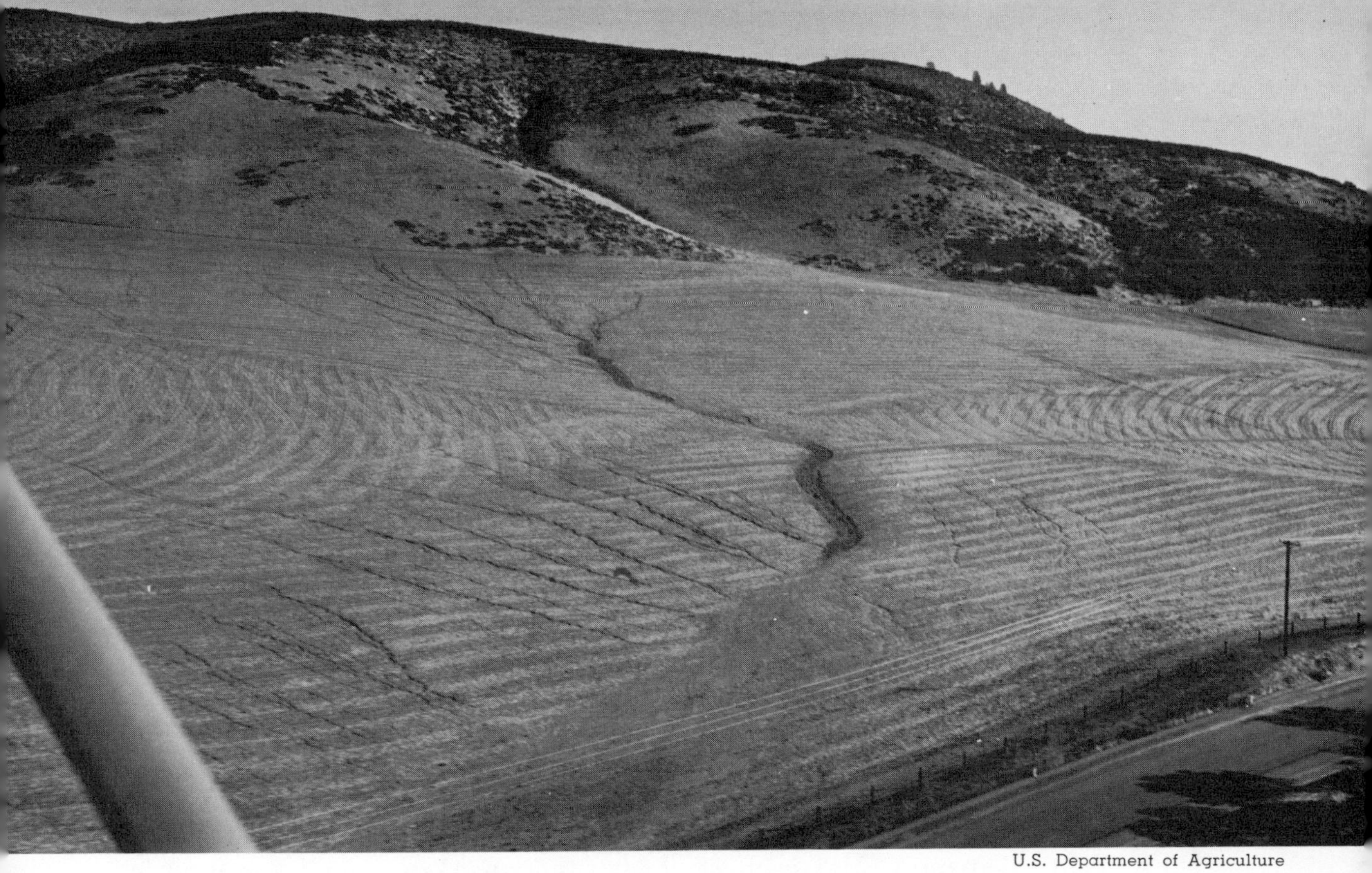

U.S. Department of Agriculture

Overworked wheat land, California.

Land planned for homes and industry without the danger of overcrowding, erosion, or pollution. Fremont, Ohio.

American Electric Power

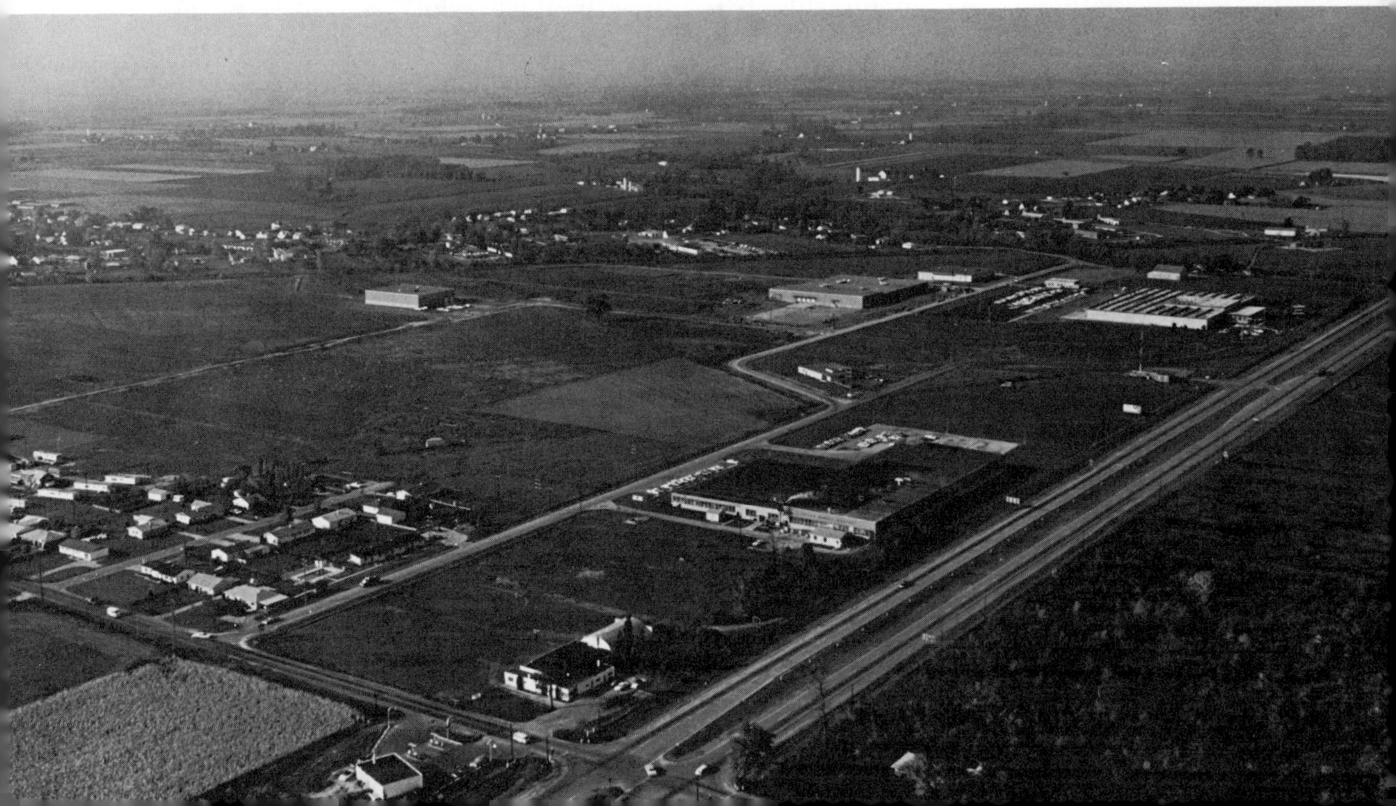

The History Of Conservation In America

America has needed a sound and active conservation program since the first tree was cut by the English colonists early in the 1600's. Some few people recognized this need and began writing and talking about it before the end of the century. Most of these early conservationists were farmers who were successful in applying conservation practices to their own land. George Washington noted erosion on his property and attempted to check it, but the widespread practice of conservation is comparatively recent.

After the Civil War caused tremendous damage to the land, people began to question if the natural resources were really limitless. It took another 25 years, however, before anything was done about it. In 1891, President Benjamin Harrison set aside the first forest reserve, Yellowstone Park Timberland Reserve. In itself this may not have been a great accomplishment, but it led the way to a national concern for the treatment of forests.

Under the administrations of Harrison and Grover Cleveland, 33 million acres of national forests were established. It was President Theodore Roosevelt, however, who made the public conscious of the need for conservation. Between 1891 and 1907, the number of acres set aside as federal lands reached 116 million. Today, the national forest system consists of 182 million acres owned and managed by the people of the United States.

State fish and game departments first attempted to conserve wildlife through hunting seasons and bag limits. The emphasis was on protecting wildlife with little or no regard to habitat improvement — the surest way to continuous wildlife crops.

The conservation of soil continued to lag. Then in the 1930's, a series of ruinous dust storms in the Great Plains area dramatically demonstrated the need for soil management. With millions of people unemployed, a public works program appeared to be the solution. President Franklin D. Roosevelt approved a program of conservation that would provide employment, revive the cause of conservation, restore some of the land, and give new strength to planning and management as national policy. The Civilian Conservation Corps, for example, used unemployed out-of-school young men in hundreds of camps throughout the land. During the 10 years of its existence three

Farm Security Administration

U.S. Forest Service

billion trees were planted, a million miles of forest roads and trails were built, 4,000 fire towers were set up, and 100,000 bridges and buildings were constructed. CCC crews turned thousands of acres into recreational land and improved more than four million acres of forest land. The work accomplished by the CCC on public lands has been estimated at more than one-and-a-half-billion dollars in value.

Through public programs of conservation administered by the United States Department of Agriculture and the United States Department of Interior, hundreds of communities have been stabilized and local economies improved; more watersheds are protected against floods; timber on many private and most public forests is cut so that there will be a continuous crop of wood; food, cover and water are recognized as the keys to more fish and wildlife; most forests are more carefully protected against fire, insects and disease. Much rangeland has been improved for domestic livestock, and great outdoor playgrounds have been made available for public use.

But the problems involved in planning for the use of our resources have moved in other directions. Today the crisis is in water. Some sections are ravaged by floods; others are parched by drought and water shortages. Most streams have been polluted and the outlook for the future is grave. Secretary of the Interior Stewart L. Udall put it this way: "Water is the conservation scandal of our generation. Water planning and water conservation must be the order of the day, even in the 'wet' regions of our country."

New Life For City And Country

Early conservation laws and activities were associated with forests and wildlands. Constructive measures were taken to prevent the nation's forests from wanton destruction, to protect wildlife from extermination, to hold back the topsoil, control floods, manage watersheds, and regulate the methods of extracting and refining minerals.

Conservation was regarded as a rural problem. Why would city dwellers be concerned with conservation when they had no acreage to manage? Now we know that conservation is a unified problem that touches the life of every citizen whether he lives in the city, a suburb, a small town, or on a farm. This view of conservation is taught us by ecology, the science that deals with the

USHA

interrelationships between living things and their environment. The word ecology comes from the Greek word *oekos,* meaning household.

Ecologists emphasize that one natural resource is related to another, and that they are all related to man. They have shown that "no man is an island," whether he lives in Chicago or rural Iowa, in well-drained Ohio or parched Arizona. The sudden, rapid spread of cities out into open areas has made conservation a universal problem. In 1900, 75 per cent of Americans lived in rural areas. Today, 75 per cent live in cities, and by the year 2,000 the figure will have risen still more.

Cities, towns, metropolitan areas — these mean highways, shopping areas, housing developments, factories, office buildings. Each year a million acres of land are swallowed up by urbanization. Nor is it any longer necessary for cities to grow near rivers, railroad terminals, or harbors as in the past. They can rise anywhere — and they do. Now is the time to determine whether

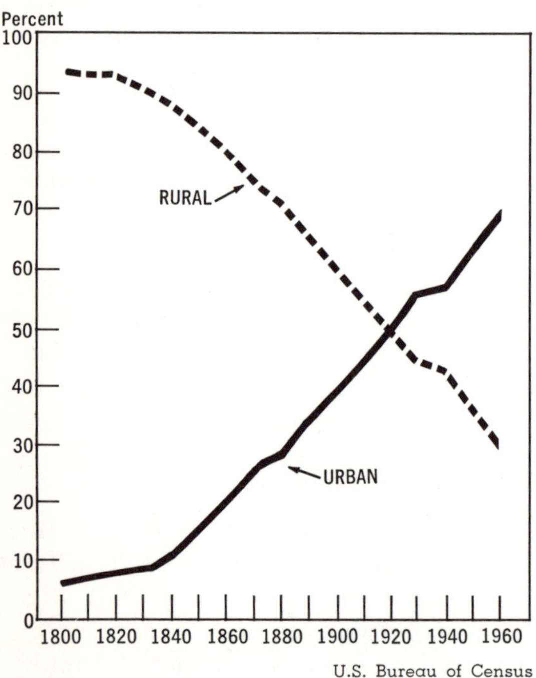

U.S. Bureau of Census

Changing proportions of rural and urban population.

USDA

A protected river valley, West Virginia.

cities will be "gray, black and brown blemishes upon green earth," or "the masterpieces of our civilization." There is much to do — clean the air and water; replace haphazard building with city planning, ugliness with beauty.

One of the great problems that confronts us is that of waste. A committee of the National Academy of Sciences submitted a report in 1966 recommending action on the haphazard treatment of all kinds of waste. The committee called it "menacing wastes." By 1980, it predicted, sewage and other wastes will absorb all the oxygen in all 22 United States river systems during dry weather. Where can cities throw the wastes without polluting air, water or land?

The committee defines waste as good material that we have not learned how to use wisely. We need a new glamour science — junk science, they tell us. Why not design cars so that the discards can be returned to the factory for re-use? Why not increase the use of water and find new uses for solid wastes? The challenge is there and it is in the hands of the land developers, city planners, engineers, industrial designers, and the federal and state governments. Ultimately, of course, it is for the people to want such planning, to be willing to pay the cost of it, and then to reap the benefits in a better way of life.

U.S. Forest Service

U.S. Department of Commerce

CHAPTER 2

U.S. Forest Service

AIR

We have taken the air we breathe for granted for so long that books on conservation of natural resources usually give air a passing mention. But that time is over. Pollution of the air — especially of the air over our cities — has reached the point where one meteorologist predicts that polluted air could put an end to life on earth within a century!

Without air we would die in a matter of minutes. The effects of polluted air are almost as serious. According to the United States Public Health Service, air pollution contributes significantly as a cause or aggravating factor to acute respiratory infection, emphysema (a lung ailment), chronic bronchitis, bronchial asthma, and lung cancer.

Air pollution is more serious when there is what meteorologists call a "temperature inversion." Ordinarily, warm air rises above cold air because it is lighter than cold air. But occasionally a layer of warm air becomes trapped beneath cold air and a higher stationary layer of cold air. In 1952, a temperature inversion kept stagnant air over London for five straight days. The poisons in the air with no place to escape accumulated and 4,000 people died. A similar condition occurred over New York City for six days in 1963 and 400 people died. The situation has since become much worse.

Pollution of our air is not new; it is just worse than it ever has been. Since man first lit a fire, he has polluted the air with soot and fumes. As early as 1306, people in London complained about air contaminated by coal-burning fires. In the centuries since then the world's air has been blackened from the smokestacks of factories and blast furnaces. Today, more than 133 million tons of filth are spewed forth each year into the air — smoke, gases, and microscopic particles of metal, oil, and grease from factories; fumes from automobiles and buses; dust and ashes from incinerators and power generators; fuel smoke from oil burners in private homes; pesticide sprays; even radioactive fallout from atomic explosions. These pollutants attack our trees, our buildings, our clothes, our furniture and utensils and — most important — our eyes and lungs. In New York City alone, air pollution costs the people $520 million each year in medical bills, cleaning and painting bills, and damage to trees, plants, fabrics, leather, books, and so on.

Air pollution is not limited to our big cities. The wide open spaces also are affected. On some days dirty air obscures the view of the Rockies from the city of Denver, Colorado. In Montana, usually known as the Land of the Big Blue Sky, there is often a "big gray sky;" death from bronchitis there has tripled in a decade and lung cancer has more than doubled. These deaths can often be traced to air pollution. This chapter describes how these things happen — and what we can do to prevent them.

Denver under smog.

Polluting Our Air

Air pollution has been defined as "the presence in the atmosphere of materials put there by the acts of people in such concentration that they interfere with people, the things people own and the things people like to do." It is most serious in our 200 largest cities. We might cite New York City once more since the problem there is now under serious consideration. On the average, 60 tons of dust, ashes, and soot fall from the air on every square mile of the city each month. Even on many clear days the Empire State Building, as seen from less than 20 blocks away, is enveloped in haze.

There are more than 250 different pollutants in the air we breathe. They are primarily products of combustion or burning — the smoke, ashes, and soot from incinerators; the sulfur dioxide from burning coal and oil furnaces; the carbon dioxide and hydrocarbons from motor vehicle engines. Smoke is the most easily seen pollutant. It combines with other elements in the air to form new pollutants.

The word *smog* was coined in 1911 to describe the dreadful mixture of smoke and fog that enveloped London and Glasgow, Scotland in that year. Actually, as we will see later, smog is more than just smoke and fog. *Smaze* is the word used to describe a combination of smoke and haze; *smust* to describe a mixture of smoke and dust.

The amount of air pollution at a given time in a given place is detected by sensitive instruments, not the least sensitive of which is your nose. But not all pollutants can be measured. For example, there is no direct way of measuring the complex hydrocarbons produced by the combustion engines of cars. Nor is there any reliable measure of the amount of pollution that can be considered "safe." The Air Pollution Index of large cities relates the amounts of sulfur dioxide and carbon monoxide in the air to the amount of visible smoke and haze. However, the remaining 25 or more pollutants are not considered in the formula. New York City defines a reading of 12 as "average" pollution and a reading of 50 as "adverse" but when 400 residents died in 1963 during a six-day temperature inversion, the Index

N.Y. Journal American

New York City.

USPHS

Los Angeles in smog.

never rose above 30. What, then, is a safe index?

It is just as difficult to measure the effects of radioactive fallout. Until the late 1950's, government and atomic science agencies assured us that radioactive fallout was not injurious beyond "a certain permissible" radiation level. We have learned since then that not even scientists can establish with certainty the biological effects of small doses of radiation. In the complicated language of one authority, it is expressed as follows: "Any increment in radiation exposure, however slight, is accompanied by a comparable increase in the risk of medically undesirable effects."

In other words, there is no absolute "safe" or "permissible" limit where pollution is concerned. All pollution may be dangerous for certain individuals, and the greater the amount of pollution the greater is the danger.

Los Angeles on a clear day.

Los Angeles County Air Pollution Control Board

Pollution From Industry

St. Louis under a blanket of smoke from factories.

There are more than 300,000 manufacturing establishments, large and small, in the United States and each one contributes in some way to air pollution. However, the main industrial pollutants are dust, smoke, odors, and chemicals.

Dust is a by-product of many industries — cement, chemical, feed and grain, iron smelting, wood, mining, and so on. The dust is caused by blasting, crushing, grinding, drying, mixing, sorting, sanding, or cutting any of the materials associated with those industries. Dust particles vary in size; the larger ones fall to the ground, the smaller ones remain in the atmosphere and restrict visibility.

Smoke is the product of burning fuels for power or heat. The smoke given out by the chimneys of private homes or apartment buildings is only a fraction of what industry contributes. Generally, smoke results from incomplete or inefficient burning. There is no reason in this day and age for air pollution to be permitted from industrial smoke. Smoke can be eliminated by the use of efficient systems for burning fuel and by smoke-control equipment.

Odors are among the most unpleasant air pollutants. Most industrial odors come from chemical plants, oil refineries, packing houses, pulp and paper factories, food processing plants, canneries, slaughter-houses, tanneries, coke ovens, and soap factories. Cities and towns add to this the stench of burning garbage. Odors are difficult to measure, control, or even to evaluate. Some people, for example, like the smell of gasoline; others are sickened by it. The same can be said of almost any odor except, perhaps, that of burning garbage or rotting substances.

You can see smoke and dust and you can smell odors, but you neither can smell nor see some of the irritating and poisonous chemical pollu-

Odors befoul the air in New York City.
Newsday

tants that industry adds to the air. One chemical pollutant that you can smell is sulfur dioxide, which forms where coal or oil is burned. These fuels contain sulfur in varying amounts — the better grades contain less — and when they burn, the sulfur combines with oxygen to form sulfur dioxide, which affects the nose, throat, and lungs of people, and the tissues of plants and trees. Sulfur dioxide also combines with tiny droplets of moisture in the air to form sulfuric acid, one of the most corrosive chemicals known. One expert estimates that we discharge into the air every day some 48,000 tons of sulfur dioxide. This deadly gas, incidentally, wastes millions of dollars worth of sulfur. Another sulfuric gas, hydrogen sulfide, peels paint off houses, walls, and automobiles.

Sulfuric gases in the air can be reduced by burning higher grade fuels or by removing the gas through special equipment. It is not economical for factories to spend money on higher grade fuels, so they would prefer to use other methods. Many oil refineries "wash" their fuel gases with pollution-control equipment that reconverts sulfuric gases to sulfur, which is then used in other ways. This is good conservation practice.

If industrial firms were to take proper conservation measures, air pollution would be reduced by 50 to 95 per cent. Many industries are working toward that goal. With the combined efforts of private citizens, government agencies, and business there is some hope that our air might be made clean again.

Pollution From Motor Vehicles

GE

C-shaped bowl, surrounded on three sides by mountains. The city's air comes from the Pacific Ocean to the west, through the opening in the C, where it is often trapped by the mountains. Temperature inversions are frequent, so that automotive pollutants — more than 8,000 tons daily of carbon monoxide alone — pile up in the atmosphere. In addition, sunlight reacts with chemicals in the auto fumes to form an irritating substance, peroxyacetyl nitrate, known as PAN. This is what is believed to cause the smarting eyes associated with smog.

Automobile fumes can be controlled. As in the burning of coal and oil, much automotive pollution

Motor vehicle exhausts rank with industrial pollutants as a major problem in air pollution. A passenger car uses a ton of air with every tankful of gasoline that it burns. In turn, it releases into the air three pounds of carbon monoxide and lesser amounts of hydrocarbons, lead, ammonia, ozone, and other corrosive gases. Jet planes give off similar pollutants in even greater quantities. Each time a jet takes off and lands it produces as much pollution as 6,800 cars!

In Los Angeles, automotive exhausts cause smog from the more than four million cars in that area. The sprawling city is situated in a

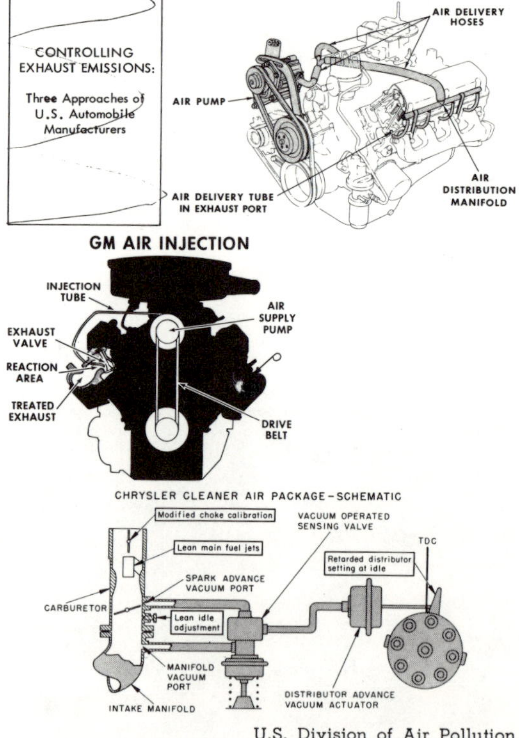

Three systems that can reduce combustion exhausts.

Leaves of trees at left were killed by exhaust fumes from buses.

is caused by incomplete combustion of fuel, in this case gasoline. A gasoline engine operates by burning a pre-mixed charge of air and gasoline vapor prepared by the carburetor. This charge is ignited by an electric spark, causing the fuel to burn. Combustion is most effective and least contaminating to the air when there is slightly less gasoline than could be burned completely with the available air. However, maximum power is attained when there is more gasoline than can burn with the available air. So, one way to cut down air pollution is to sacrifice power — speed and acceleration — for more effective combustion. Unfortunately, this has not been done nor is it likely to be done until the public realizes that health and safety are more important than highly-publicized horsepower.

Automotive pollutants come from four sources — the tail pipe, the carburetor, the fuel tank, and the crankcase. Only the crankcase pollutants are not adequately controlled. All new cars manufactured since 1964 in the United States carry a device that directs unburned fuel vapors, largely hydrocarbons, back to the carburetor. California law has required this device on all new cars for several years and, by 1968, it will be required by federal law. Unfortunately, however, the federal law does not provide for periodic inspection of this device, which means the controls eventually could prove worthless.

These devices cut automotive air pollution by 50 per cent. But this is not enough. Legal measures cover only new cars so that it will be at least ten years before even a majority of the cars on the road are equipped. Meanwhile, by 1990, the number of cars on the road is expected to double. If we have half the pollution but double the number of polluting vehicles, then we are merely standing still — in dirty air.

Automobile manufacturers and local, state, and federal pollution-control agencies are carrying on research to find better ways of preventing contamination. A program of public education also is needed to show how automobiles can be run with greater efficiency and with less danger to health.

Control Of Air Pollution

In 1299, King Edward I of England hanged one of his subjects for polluting the air with black smoke from a coal fire. Until recently, however, air pollution has not been considered a serious problem except in heavily industrial cities. But this complacency is changing. An accumulation of neglect in the United States has made air pollution a vital issue of the 1960's. Spurred by the destruction of life, nature, and property caused by dirty air, Americans are taking steps to control pollution at the source.

Air pollution control is complex and costly, but it is possible. Twenty-five years ago the sun rarely shone through in Pittsburgh. It could not pierce the dense clouds of smoke which poured from the stacks of the steel mills. Sixty tons of soot fell every month on every square mile of the "Smoky City." Then, in 1946, the city government, with strong support from citizens' action groups, began a campaign to clean the skies over Pittsburgh.

Industry was persuaded to install smoke abatement equipment. House-

So. Calif. Edison

Air pollution control built into a steam generating plant.

holders were restricted in their burning of garbage. Within only ten years there was a reduction of almost 90 per cent in the smoke over the city. Poor visibility hours were reduced from 1,000 to less than 75. Because air pollution affects large areas, the smoke control program in Pittsburgh was coordinated with that of Allegheny County in 1958. Under the expanded program, 95 per cent of industrial air pollution may be eliminated by 1971. Pittsburgh today is a gleaming, prosperous, beau-

Pittsburgh before control. USPHS

Pittsburgh after control. USPHS

Testing pollution from a factory by the effects on cotton cloth strips.

tiful city — and the key to its recovery is its control of air pollution.

Los Angeles was forced to take steps to reduce serious air pollution. A state law was passed to prohibit the people of Los Angeles from burning garbage or leaves. Rigid standards for the control of certain automotive exhausts were established. The city also compelled electric power stations to convert from oil to natural gas as the source of fuel. Industrial plants were required to use air pollution control equipment.

All over the country, cities and towns are waking up to the problem of air pollution. Thirty-three states now have some kind of air pollution control laws. Most of these laws, however, do not go far enough or are not enforced. Actually the problem of air pollution is too complex for the cities or states to solve by themselves. Air respects no political or geographic boundaries. It may become polluted in one place and blow over to another area. For this reason, the federal government is strengthening controls by assisting local and state pollution-control agencies.

A limited program of research was authorized by Congress in 1955 under the Air Pollution Control Act administered by the United States Public Health Service. In 1963, the Clean Air Act was passed. This enabled the federal government to offer funds and technical assistance to state and local agencies. The Department of Interior provides some control over interstate pollution problems. The Clean Air Act sets standards for automotive exhausts and provides funds for additional research. Much more help is needed, for this is only the beginning. What is your community doing in the campaign for clean air — and what are you doing to help?

U.S. Forest Service

CHAPTER 3

WATER

After air, our most important resource is water. We can live only a few minutes without air, only a few days without water.

We drink water, swim and bathe in it, catch fish from it, grow crops with it, and use it to generate electricity and to manufacture most of our products. Science and technology depend on vast quantities of water to carry on research and the chances are that water use will continue to expand. We know vaguely that water is essential to life, but with few exceptions, we take it for granted. When we turn on the tap, it flows. Recent experience, however, has shown that we no longer can take water for granted.

A combination of prolonged drought, rapid industrial expansion, and population growth has created a critical water shortage in the United States and in other countries throughout the world. A five-year drought in the northeastern section of our country left the land parched, the reservoirs dry, and the streams slowed down to a trickle. Industrial wastes and untreated urban sewage have polluted streams, rivers, and lakes. "The southern tip of Lake Michigan," a United States Senator has observed, "is turning into a cesspool." Lake Erie, because of pollution, is called a "dead lake."

This is a time of crisis in water.

The crisis threatens to grow worse. Today, Americans use *355 billion gallons of water each day!* By 1980, we will need 587 billion gallons daily, and by the year 2000 we will need 969 billion gallons. Where will we get it? There is no more water on earth today than there was billions of years ago when the planet was formed; nor is the supply likely to increase. The only answer is water conservation. It has been recommended that we try to hold every drop of water where it falls. "If you can't do that, make it walk off instead of run off."

Strangely enough, water is one of our most abundant resources. It covers more than 70 per cent of the earth's surface. If the water of the oceans were poured evenly over the dry land surface covering the globe, it would bury the land everywhere 800 feet deep. The trouble is that all this water is salty — unfit in its natural state to use for drinking, irrigation, or industry. More than 97 per cent of the earth's water is in the oceans. Another two per cent lies frozen and useless in glaciers and icecaps. The tiny fraction of usable water that remains is neither evenly distributed nor properly used. We will see in this chapter what has been done with water resources and what needs to be done to assure a supply for present and future generations.

The Water Cycle

The water we use has been here ever since the earth was formed billions of years ago. Water does not get "used up," but it circulates endlessly in a cycle.

There is no beginning to a cycle, but, for the sake of convenience, let us say that the water cycle begins with the evaporation of water from the oceans. This vast amount of water usually is measured in cubic miles — a cubic mile being equal to 1,101,117,143,000 gallons. The oceans contain 317 million cubic miles of water. The sun evaporates 230 million cubic miles of this amount into the atmosphere daily;

210 million fall back into the sea in some form of precipitation (rain or snow), and 20 million cubic miles are blown over land by the prevailing winds. In the United States these winds generally blow from west to east.

At the same time, 50 million cubic miles of water are evaporated into the atmosphere from the land, from lakes, rivers, and plants. The water vapor released by plants enters the atmosphere through the process of transpiration by which the plant "breathes out" moisture through its leaves. An acre of corn, for example, transpires about 4,000 gallons of water a day. One of the problems of water conservation is how to reduce or capture the amount of water lost through evaporation and transpiration.

The 70 million cubic miles of water — 20 from the ocean and 50 from the land — fall on land as rain or snow, completing the cycle. The water that falls on land distributes itself in several ways. About 35 million cubic miles go into rivers, streams, and lakes; 20 million run off the land and back into the oceans; and about 16 million seep down through the soil to keep the soil moist and to replenish the supply of ground water, known as aquifers.

We don't know as much as we would like to about aquifers. We know only that great supplies of water, perhaps 2 million cubic feet, may flow through the rocks below the surface of the earth. Its uppermost level is known as the *water table*. This may be several feet or several thousand feet below the earth's surface, depending upon location. In some places in Saudi Arabia, the water table is 3,500 feet below the surface, and it costs $250,000 to drill a well for water.

If aquifers are not replenished, the water table falls. In Phoenix, Arizona, which draws much of the water from underground wells, the water table drops eight feet each year. This is another of the many problems that must be considered in planning for the use of water.

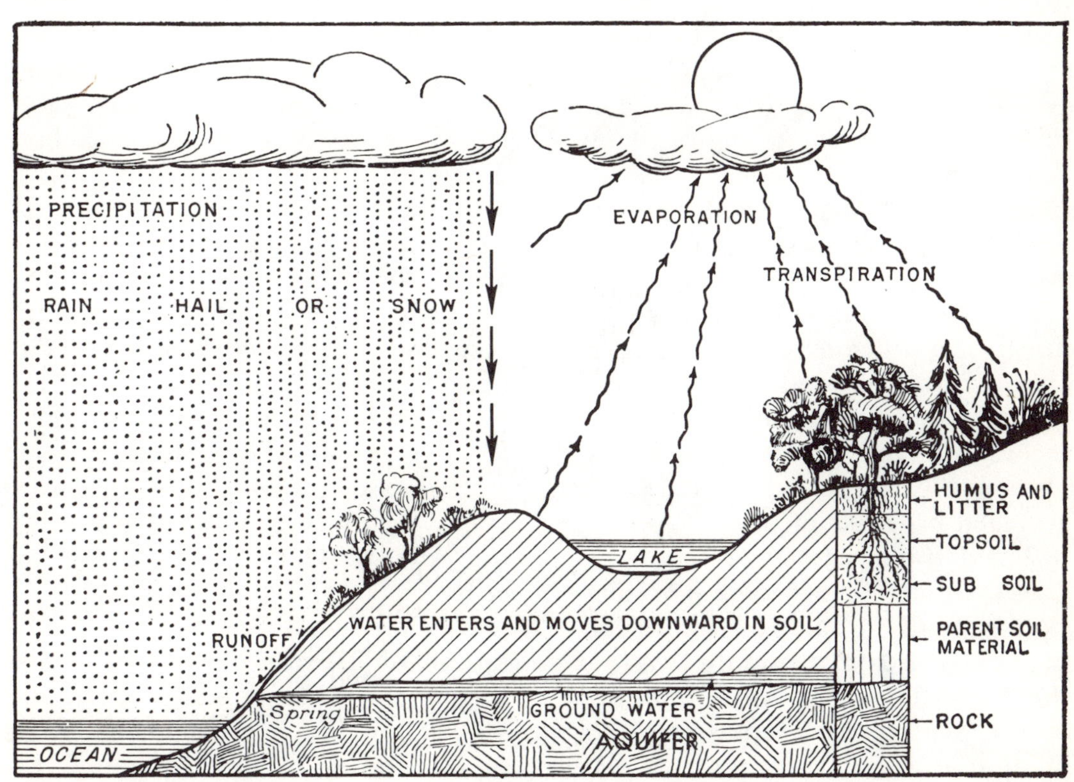

U.S. Forest Service

Drought And Flood

USDA

Drought and poor farming combine to destroy
a home and livelihood.

USD

Poor drainage and improper farming
cause floods and disaster.

The rain that falls in the water cycle does not, unfortunately, fall everywhere in equal amounts. Too little rain may cause drought in New York, while at the same time too much rain may cause floods in Minnesota. Each place on earth receives a certain amount of precipitation every year; the amount does not vary much over the years. For example, over a 74-year period, Cherra Punji in India received an average of 450 inches of precipitation annually. Over a 43-year period, Arica, Chile averaged only .02 inches.

The United States as a whole averages about 30 inches of precipitation annually. But, roughly speaking, one-third of this falls west of the Mississippi, two-thirds falls east of the Mississippi. The amount of precipitation can vary from place to

place within a few hundred miles. Precipitation in Wenatchee, Washington is 151 inches and Greenland Ranch, California only 1.5 inches. There are many reasons for this. Mountain ranges, which collect rain from the air passing over them, leave the air dry for the rest of the area. Air currents may mysteriously change directions. The air currents that normally bring rain to the eastern seacoast of the United States, for example, for some unexplained reason, shifted eastward for a few years, carrying the normal rainfall out over the Atlantic Ocean and leaving the coastal populations in a drought.

The area served by the Metropolitan Water District of Southern California must bring water to almost 10,000,000 people living at the edge of a near-desert. An aqueduct, reminiscent of those built by the Romans 1,500 years ago on another continent, carries water 242 miles from the Colorado River across desert, through mountain ranges, and hundreds of miles of pipe to 119 cities and towns of Los Angeles, Orange, Riverside, San Bernardino, San Diego, and Ventura counties. Another network planned by the State of California will reach Southern California, over a distance of 450 miles from the Sacramento and San Joaquin rivers, through dams, reservoirs, canals, tunnels, and pipelines.

These long-distance pipelines, together with planned desalination projects, will probably take care of the future needs of a state that may double its population by 1990.

If too much rain or snow falls in one area, floods result. The rivers and streams simply cannot hold the extra water within their channels so they overflow. Sometimes, even when the snowfall has been normal, unusually warm weather will cause a flood by melting the snow too quickly. A combination of heavy snowfall and early melting can be disastrous. In the spring of 1965,

the upper Mississippi watersheds (areas of land that shed water into streams) held an unusually heavy winter's snowfall. Early warm weather, combined with heavy rains, converted this snow rapidly to water — more than the stream channels could carry. The water, impeded by ice floes, increased in volume as it flowed downstream and picked up more water from the smaller tributary streams along the way. By the time it reached Minneapolis and St. Paul, the river was in flood and caused millions of dollars in damage.

Man can only do so much to prevent a flood such as this one. He can make sure that the watersheds are planted in trees and grass or crops in such a way that the water does not run off quickly. He can build dikes and levees, small check dams and storage reservoirs, and he can straighten and dredge river channels. This will prevent many small floods. But every once in a while, it may be every 100 years, a heavy flood will occur that cannot be held back. That is why people who live on flood plains are advised to build their houses high — or move out.

Metropolitan Water District of Southern California.

Watersheds

No matter where water falls on land, there is a watershed to receive it. A watershed is a combination of hills, valleys, streams, ponds, forests, grass, crops, and soil all draining into a common basin. But it also includes cities, towns, roads, airports, recreation areas, factories, railroads, homes, people, and animals.

Poor water management brings waste and poverty.

Until the close of World War II, watershed was a term used mainly by scientists, conservationists, and engineers. After the war, people became more concerned with water needs and water problems and the word gradually came into common use. Many people now understand that a watershed is an area of land from which the streams, lakes, aquifers, swamps, and marshes get their supplies of water.

A watershed may be as large as several states or smaller than a single building lot. Rain or melting snow often form small puddles. The area around each puddle is a tiny watershed where any water on it flows toward the lowest point. The Mississippi River watershed of 1.25 million square miles of land is a combination of thousands of smaller watersheds that collect rain and snow water and feed it into successively larger watersheds until it finally reaches the main river. Watersheds are useful as land for grazing, planting, or building. But these activities must be carefully controlled. Many watersheds produce only water — which is valuable enough.

Conservation is especially necessary on the higher, steeper, and rougher watersheds, most of which are wild lands, forests, range, or hillside farms. These watersheds receive more rain and snow than the lower lands; yet they have the steepest slopes and thinnest soils. They are easily damaged by erosion and where plant cover is thin, water cannot go

East Willow Creek Watershed, Minnesota. Note the dam and good farming methods that hold down rain water and soil.

into the ground. The resulting fast runoff causes floods. But when good conservation practices are applied to watersheds, most of the water that falls soaks into the ground, where nature slowly releases it to the streams.

A watershed in good condition gives a steady flow of water. Sometimes, however, even in good watersheds the water may rage out of control. This is what happened in 1965 when floods of the Mississippi River caused great damage in Minnesota, Wisconsin, Illinois, Iowa, and Missouri.

Watersheds in poor condition offer no protection against floods. For example, brush fires in 1964 destroyed the protective plant cover of the watersheds near Los Angeles, California. In the spring of 1965, the whole watershed system, without plants, broke down. Rain drops pounded the bare soil and formed little rivulets which got bigger and bigger on their way downhill. The topsoil was washed away and deposited on homes, businesses, streets, lawns, and parks causing great personal and community loss.

A watershed in good condition is a beautiful sight. There is a thick plant cover of grass, trees, and shrubs and the soil is spongy. Streams flow the year round, protecting the land from fire. Logging is planned carefully to prevent erosion and to keep the forest productive. The banks of road cuts and railroad tracks are protected with plants. Farmers use good conservation practices to keep the water on the land and to prevent the loss of soil.

U.S. Bureau of Public Roads

Recreation area in a watershed.

A sick watershed, however, looks pitiful. There is little or no cover on the ground and little humus in the soil. Usually fires have damaged or killed trees and other plants. Some soil is bare, some weedy. Small and large gullies appear on the slopes of the hills. Stream banks are eroding, stream channels are silted, and streams are muddy or dry. Everyone, city dwellers included, suffers from a poorly managed watershed.

The Watershed Protection and Flood Prevention Act helps to bridge the hurdle between the knowledge and technical assistance available through the United States Department of Agriculture and the many landowners and operators who want to participate but find it too expensive. The federal government works with local organizations and state agencies to build dams, aqueducts, and recreational areas as part of watershed management and flood control. Farmers and ranchers share part of the cost and practice contour planting, strip cropping, and woodlot management.

Fresh Water

U.S. Forest Service

Fresh water is the only water suitable for drinking, for irrigating crops, and for industrial uses. In the United States, most fresh water is surface water. It comes from streams, rivers, reservoirs, and lakes. Reservoirs, of which there are more than 10,000, store runoff water until it is needed by cities, towns, farmers, industry, or electric power plants.

If the watersheds are carefully managed and precipitation is normal, streams deliver steady water supplies to the storage reservoirs. Unfortunately, in too many cases, conservation practices on these watersheds are either inadequate or entirely lacking, so streamflow is irregular and water supplies fluctuate. Careless timber harvesting, forest fires, poor farming methods, overgrazing, poor road location and construction — all have a harmful effect on watersheds and, therefore, on stream flow. So,

USDA

A reservoir in a watershed area, Arizona. Silt washed into the reservoir causes clogging.

the first step in the conservation of water is to apply sound forestry and soil conservation practices. The second step is to avoid polluting the water.

Drinking water that comes from a river, lake, or, reservoir must be treated chemically to make it safe. This is done at a treatment plant where chemicals are added to the water to remove impurities, kill harmful bacteria, destroy bad tastes or odors and, if necessary, make the water softer and less rust-forming. After a period in sedimentation basins, the chemically treated impurities settle to the bottom. The water is then filtered through large sand and gravel troughs to strain out the remaining impurities. Then, before it goes into the water system, the water is treated with chlorine to kill any harmful bacteria still remaining.

Underground aquifers are the other major source of fresh water. They provide about a sixth of all water used in the United States. These aquifers are fed by rain and snow water that seeps through the ground. Ground water may come to the surface as springs, but most of it is pumped up from drilled wells.

Sometimes underground pressure forces the water to the surface once a well is drilled. This is known as an artesian well. Florida has thousands of artesian wells. More often, however, ground water must be pumped to the surface. If the water table drops, wells must be dug deeper to reach it.

Most of the water for rural homes comes from the ground through wells and springs. Some cities, like Phoenix, Arizona, get most of their water from wells. As with surface water, ground water can best be conserved by taking good care of the watershed. Avoiding quick runoff is particularly important. If little rain falls on the watershed, as happens in Arizona, then other sources of water must be found or tapped to supplement the underground wells, and the water supply must be managed carefully. This is the challenge of the 1960's — to manage the limited supplies of fresh water for the growing population of the nation and the entire world.

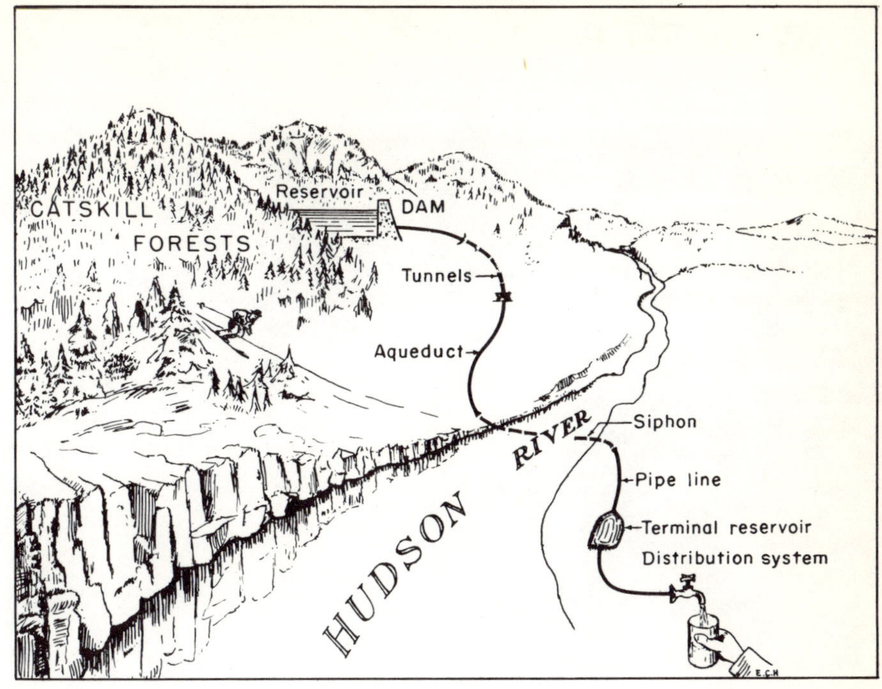

U.S. Forest Service

A city water supply system.

Water For People

How do we do it? We use water for showers and sanitation, for air coolers and heaters, automatic clothes and dish washers. An ordinary shower requires 12 gallons of water — more than all the water you would have used in three days a century ago. We have many other uses for water in our times — to sprinkle the lawn or garden, fill the swimming pool, and wash the car. In some cities where water is scarce, these less important uses of water have to be regulated.

Under normal conditions people need about three quarts of drinking water daily. If each person were to increase his activity, he would need more; if he were to remain quiet and inactive, he would need less.

Water for drinking is, of course, our most important need. But we use water in many other ways, too. One hundred years ago if you had lived in the country or in a small town, your family would have used perhaps three or four gallons of water per day per person for all its needs — drinking, cooking, bathing, and washing clothes. Now most Americans live in cities and use about 180 gallons of water per person each day! This takes into account the water used for sanitation, fire protection, as well as water used by industry.

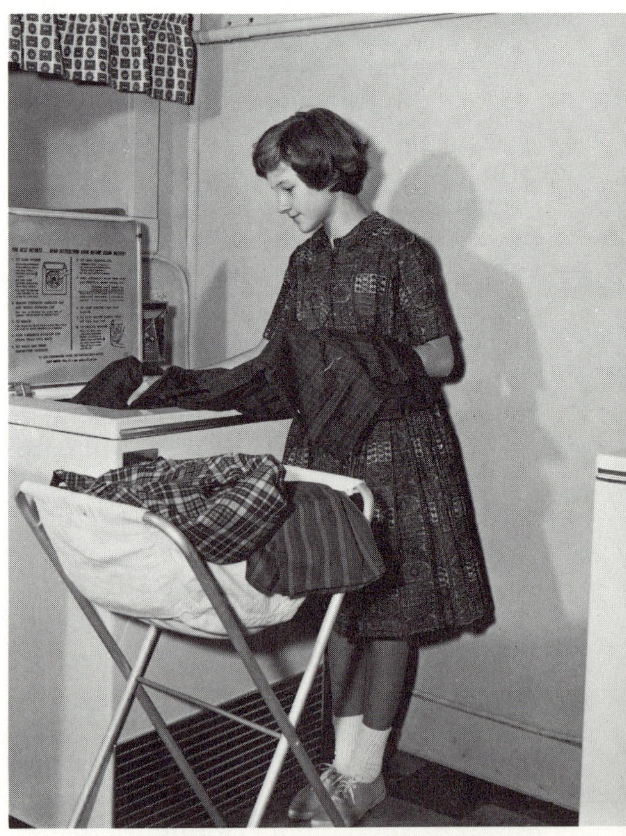

Cornell University College of Home Econ.

These are just the uses for water in the home. Water is also important for recreation, as in swimming, fishing, and boating. Where natural lakes are not available, streams are dammed to provide lakes or ponds. In designing reservoirs for electric power production, flood control or river regulation, the planners usually make provision for the recreational use of water. For example, a dam 25 feet high may be adequate for flood control on a small watershed. To be of value for boating and fishing, a height of 35 feet would be needed. So a 35-foot dam is built and what would have been a single-use water structure becomes one of multiple use, with a saving in cost.

Not long ago, to suggest the public use of a municipal water supply reservoir or its watershed would have caused a public debate. Today, modern sanitation engineering makes it possible to permit boating, fishing, even swimming in many large reservoirs. In addition, the people enjoy the surrounding lands for picnicking, camping, winter sports, hunting, and other types of outdoor recreation. Such activities indicate the new trend in our thinking about water, when all our needs are considered in water management.

Water For Agriculture

USDA

A power sprinkler system irrigates a corn crop, Oregon.

Agriculture, t h e production of crops and livestock, requires just about one-half of all the fresh water used in the United States each year. The water that is not provided by precipitation must be provided by irrigation, in which water is brought to the crops from a distant source. Irrigation accounts for most of the water used in farming. It takes up to 750,000 gallons of water to irrigate one acre of farm land.

Irrigation has been known to man for thousands of years. Excavated ruins have revealed ancient water tanks and irrigation canals or ditches built more than 5,000 years ago in the Indus Valley of India. A rock-filled dam in Egypt stored water for irrigation 50 centuries ago. Almost a thousand years before the Christian Era, King Solomon ordered the con-struction of aqueducts to provide water for "man, beast and field."

Dams still help to control water for irrigation. In most systems the water for irrigation is delivered to the crops entirely by gravity. Canals take the water from large streams or dammed reservoirs (often many miles away) and distribute it through smaller artificial water-courses called irrigation ditches. When it reaches the gently sloping fields, the water moves by gravity to small ditches between the rows of crops. If water pressures are high enough, the water may be spread through sprinkler systems.

Where surface water is inadequate or too far away for gravity irrigation, underground wells are used. Irrigation from well water may be adequate by gravity flow after the water has been brought to the surface or by sprinkler where adequate pressures can be built up by pumps.

Irrigation w a t e r also may be pumped d i r e c t l y from nearby streams, lakes, or reservoirs. This is done in the eastern part of the United States where irrigation, m o s t l y t h r o u g h sprinklers, relieves the farmer from total dependence on natural rainfall.

Irrigation is a "consumptive" use of water. This means that most water used for agriculture goes back into the atmosphere through plant transpiration and natural evaporation. This process is known technically as *evapotranspiration,* a combination of the words evaporation and transpiration. Scientists are carefully studying how much water crops need so that surplus water will not be lost in transpiration. One method that has been tried is to spray a heavy chemical over the surface of a lake or reservoir to prevent evaporation. But the wind may blow the chemical toward the shore, leaving most of the water uncovered.

Large dams play an important part in water conservation. They generate electric power for nearby communities, provide water for irrigation and for drinking, create lakes for boating, fishing, and camping. Dams are also used to control the flow of rivers. The dams built for the Tennessee Valley Authority stopped the frequent floods and turned a depressed, poverty-stricken valley into an electrified and productive region that combined agriculture and industry. The great western dams, such as Hoover and Grand Coulee, have brought millions of acres of desert land under cultivation through irrigation, while providing a source of hydroelectric power. Dams are being built throughout the world to control the supply of water.

Conservationists believe that some dams destroy wilderness areas and wildlife habitats and might have been located elsewhere. They also point out that great amounts of water are lost by evaporation when large lakes are formed. Of course, people do not always agree on what is good and what is harmful, and a great deal of debate and discussion accompany all large engineering projects no matter what their purpose.

Gravity irrigation through siphon tubes, Texas.

Water For Industry

Smith Mountain Dam on the Roanoke River, Virginia.

Despite the many ways in which individuals use water, families use only 10 per cent of the nation's consumption of this precious resource. We have seen that 50 per cent goes for agriculture; and the remaining 40 per cent is used by industry.

Industry's need for water is vast and it is increasing. Water is used to produce many products and, in the past, little attention was given to conserving the amount used. For example, 200 gallons of water are needed to yield a dollar's worth of paper, 770 gallons to refine a barrel of petroleum, 65,000 gallons to manufac-

ture one automobile, 320,000 gallons to produce a ton of aluminum. Every time a jet passenger plane takes off, 1,000 gallons of water are used, and to launch an ICBM rocket requires 500,000 gallons of water.

Unlike the water used in agriculture, industrial water can be used again and again. Most of the water used in farming returns to the atmosphere through evapotranspiration, but water used in industry is returned to streams and the ground. A large manufacturing plant may draw water from a river upstream and, after using it for cooling, wash-

ing, power production and processing, the remaining water goes back
to the river a few hundred yards
downstream. The problem is that
this water may not be clean; in fact,
it is often filled with chemicals that
pollute the entire river and destroy
the plants and fish that live there.

Industries depend upon water and
they must also cooperate in keeping
water suitable for all other uses in
communities. The R u h r River,
which flows through West Germany's
most concentrated industrial region,
is clean enough for boating and swimming even in the shadow of smokestacks. This is because 2,200 industries and 250 municipalities cooperate in keeping pollution under control. Each industry must purify the
water it uses before returning it to
the river. The steel industry, for example, recirculates the water it uses.
As a result, it has cut its use of the
Ruhr River water by 98 per cent.

The power-generating industry
does not change the nature of water.
To generate electricity r e q u i r e s
seven times more water than is used
for all other purposes, but practically
all of the water is returned in its
original state. Its temperature may
rise as it goes through the generators,
but otherwise its quality remains un-
changed. The problem becomes one
of keeping the temperature at a level
that will not destroy fish and aquatic
plants.

Power production uses more water
in the United States than the 1,200
billion gallons, but most of it is immediately returned to the streams
for other uses.

This generator in the Cardinal Plant on
the Ohio River can generate 600,000 kilo-
watts of electricity.

One engineer can monitor automated
equipment in a power plant.

Polluted Water

Shenandoah River,
Virginia

Va. Fisheries Commission

Water pollution is already infiltrating most of the fresh water supply in the nation. "We are living in our own filth," a government official said. That is literally true. Every river system in America has been polluted to some extent. The Great Lakes, which hold 30 per cent of the world's supply of fresh water, have been transformed into a "chemical tank." New York's majestic and historic Hudson River, whose shoreline touches the lives of 10 million people, is an "open sewer." The Potomac River carries a stream of "decaying sewage and rotten algae" past the nation's capital.

How has this been allowed to happen? About two-thirds of all pollution is caused by industry, which pours into streams and lakes a combination of oil, grease, chemicals, pulp, detergents, acids, slaughterhouse wastes, and factory refuse. The rest is caused by raw or poorly treated sewage dumped by towns and cities. This sewage includes wastes from bathtubs, toilets, sinks, laundries,

Federal Water Pollution Control Admin.

The light area shows pollution in the Cleveland harbor.

46

chicken farms, restaurants, hospitals, hotels, mortuaries, swimming pools — anything that goes into a sewer system. Pollution also is caused by boats and cargo ships that discharge their wastes directly into lakes, and by the pesticides that cling to soil as it is carried into the waters.

Pollution has a very serious effect on the balance of nature in streams and lakes. It breeds disease, carries wastes far and wide over the countryside, and blights the waterways. It lowers property values, destroys jobs, and reduces recreation facilities.

Water pollution can be controlled at the source. Once it has been introduced, it can be eliminated, though the cost of elimination is much greater than that of prevention. One example of pollution control may be cited. For years the Ohio River was everybody's sewer and nobody's responsibility. Fewer than one per cent of the millions of people and hundreds of industries along its banks made any attempt to treat the sewage and wastes. Then, in 1948, eight states served by the river — Illinois, Indiana, Kentucky, Ohio, Pennsylvania, New York, Virginia, and West Virginia — created the Ohio River Valley Water Sanitation Commission. The commission included representatives of the federal government as

East Liverpool (Ohio) Review

Monitoring water pollution control, Ohio Valley Water Sanitation Program.

well as of the eight states. Its goal was "to prevent pollution by sewage or industrial wastes . . . . from seriously affecting the various uses of interstate waters." Today, practically all sewage is treated and much of the industrial waste has been curbed. The Ohio River is not yet clean, but it is far better than it was before the Commission began its work.

Since 1956, the Federal Water Pollution Control Act made federal funds available to industries that built waste treatment plants. In 1965, Congress passed a Water Quality Act to establish a national policy for the prevention, control, and abatement of water pollution. This law was made necessary because waterways cross state boundaries and it was recognized that control had to be regulated by the federal government. The Act encourages joint federal, state, and local action, for without local cooperation the program would fail. Grants are given for waste treatment plants, for research on all aspects of water pollution, and for enforcement of water quality standards.

Rock River, Illinois.

Chicago Tribune

Re-using Water

Sludge from the four circular ponds is pumped to the tanks (foreground) for t r e a t m e n t, Washington.

Community management of water use is a new idea in the United States. One aspect of it is to tap the natural sources of water in the water cycle. But management goes beyond that. It seeks to short-circuit the water cycle, that is, to get pure water without waiting for the entire cycle to operate. There are several ways of doing this. One is by desalting water, discussed later. Another, and more important way in our highly technological society, is to use water more than once.

One hydrologist, or water expert, expressed it this way: "We think in terms of using water once and then throwing it away. But there is no more reason for throwing away water because it's dirty than there is for throwing away a shirt because it's dirty. Both can be cleaned." Today many industries in the United States recirculate the water they use.

More than 400 years ago, the citizens of Bunzlau in Silesia conserved water by spreading sewage on nearby farmland. The idea of using processed sewage or "waste water" for drinking or swimming is repugnant to many people. This is because they do not know the facts. Sea water contains three times as much contamination as sewage. Sewage actually is 99 per cent plain water, with only about one per cent of it being pollutants. There are ways of processing the one per cent to make the water purer than when it came from the spring.

Residents of Los Angeles, a city which has a chronic water problem because Southern California has so little rainfall, now gets processed water as part of their drinking water. Fresh water is piped in from the Colorado River 200 miles away and poured over "spreading beds" on the outskirts of the city to percolate down and replenish the aquifers that supply the city's wells. Along with this fresh water, 17 million gallons a day of processed "waste" water is sprinkled over the spreading beds to percolate d o w n to the aquifers.

Chemically, this waste water is purer than the water drawn from the Colorado River.

A similar project was undertaken by Pennsylvania State University in 1962. The university, instead of discharging its treated sewage into a creek (as it had been doing), spread it over open fields of cropland and woods. Within three years the fall of the water table had been reduced from 75 feet a year to just a few feet; the crop yields in the sprinkled fields trebled, and its protein content increased. Trees grew faster and birds and animals thrived.

Processed water does not need to be used as the main source of drinking water. There are so many other uses for it that it releases the supplies of fresh water for drinking. For example, in Las Vegas, Nevada; Santa Fe, New Mexico; and San Francisco, California processed waste

Federal Water Pollution Control Admin.

Aerating river water in a settling basin.

water is used to sprinkle golf courses; in San Antonio, Texas it is used to irrigate crops.

We have turned to the idea of re-using water just in time, for if we had not, we might have exhausted our supply of available water within a generation.

Dried sludge is used as fertilizer.

Federal Water Pollution Control Admin.

Re-using water in an oil refinery, Texas.

Federal Water Pollution Control Admin.

Salt Water To Fresh

The Greek philosopher, Aristotle, noted 2,300 years ago that when salt water turned into vapor it became sweet and the vapor did not form salt water again when it condensed. This, of course, is what happens in part of the water cycle. Sunlight evaporates water vapor from the sea, it condenses and falls to earth again as fresh rain or snow. Man has been trying to duplicate this process for centuries.

He has had some success. Julius Caesar distilled water from the sea for his legions to drink during the siege of Alexandria. Ancient mariners boiled sea water to condense fresh drinking water. Today, United States Navy vessels and many ocean liners carry desalination units with which they convert salt water to fresh water. But, for general use, desalting sea water is still very costly.

There are several ways of desalinating water. The simplest method is used on the tiny Greek island of Syme. Sea water is placed in long troughs and the fresh water vapor evaporated by the sun's heat is collected. But this would be impractical in areas where there was less sun or a greater demand for water.

A practical method is used at the Red Sea port of Eilat in Israel. The salt water is frozen in a special plant. In freezing, the ice crystals form separately from the brine, then melt down as fresh water. This method was developed by Alexander Zarchin, who as a youth in Siberia noticed that he could drink melted water from the ice of salty seas.

The most common method in use is to distill sea water in huge plants. The water is sprayed into a low-pressure chamber, where heat flashes it into steam, which is drawn off and sprayed into a series of similar chambers; the process is repeated there until perhaps one gallon of fresh water has been condensed from 3.5 gallons of salt water. This water is so pure that if it is not mixed with fresh water, it will remove scale and rust from pipes and plumbing and again contaminate itself.

There are more than 200 water distilling plants around the world from Kuwait on the Persian Gulf to Guantanamo Bay, Cuba. The chief problem in flash distillation, or in any desalination method, is producing the fresh water cheaply. Engineers have brought the cost down from $5 per thousand gallons of water to about one dollar. But it must come down to less than 35¢ per thousand gallons to make it economically worthwhile for general use.

The principal cost of desalination is the power to run the machinery. One of the advantages of Zarchin's freezing method is that it takes less power to freeze than to heat. In crowded Hong Kong, a desalination plant is powered by burning garbage! Other power sources have been tried, including electricity and natural gas. Nuclear power plants are planned for Long Island, New York and Los Angeles. The latter plant will produce 150 million gallons of fresh water daily.

The United States government is financing research on water desalination in our own country, in Israel, and other lands. The prediction is that by the year 2,000 seven per cent of America's water will be distilled from the sea.

Catalina Island, California conversion plant.

So. Cal. Edison

Westinghouse

Guantanomo Bay produces electric power as well as fresh water.

Westinghouse

Salt water to fresh by evaporation, then condensation, St. Thomas, Virgin Islands.

Israel Information Service

At Eilat, Israel salt water is frozen and the ice crystals that form are washed and evaporated to produce fresh water. This is the Zarchin process.

International Spotlight On Water

While engineers seek ways of making desalination more economical, many hydrologists are carrying out research to find ways of getting more water out of the natural water cycle. This is the purpose of a ten-year study, begun in 1966, called the International Hydrological Decade.

The IHD is modeled after the International Geophysical Year of 1957-58, which led to the launching of the first earth satellites. One of the mysteries the IHD will attempt to solve is what happens to a sizable amount of water which is unaccountably lost from the continents each year. Hydrologists estimate the water loss in the United States to be 40 cubic miles per year — almost one-third of the vast outflow of the Mississippi River.

How is this water lost? Nobody knows. But hydrologists suspect that it is lost somehow through underground routes. Most of the world's supply of fresh water is held in underground aquifers. One of the most encouraging developments in water conservation has been the success in replenishing these aquifers. We have seen how this was done with waste water in Los Angeles and at Pennsylvania State University. There are also ways of doing it through the use of the natural water cycle.

For example, heavy farming was steadily depleting the aquifers of the San Dimas Basin between Los Angeles and San Bernardino, California until hydrologists devised a conservation plan for the area. Much of the water from the winter rain and snow was flowing uselessly out to sea via the area's rivers. "Spreading works" were built where the rivers ran from the mountains to the plains. These structures backed up the water and allowed it to spread over the gravel beds through which it could percolate d o w n w a r d to the aquifers. Streams were diverted into deep wells or into dry stream beds. Together, these measures succeeded in raising the water table to within 85 feet of ground level. This form of fresh water storage is practiced in many urban coastal areas in our own and other countries.

Under the International Hydrological Decade, hydrologists throughout the world will continue to seek new ways of adding more usable water to the world's supply, perhaps by finding ways to check evaporation from lakes and reservoirs. Water is one of the most critical problems on earth, one where better management and conservation are absolutely essential. The IHD may prove to be "the most important long-range international program yet organized to help make human knowledge serve human welfare."

UN

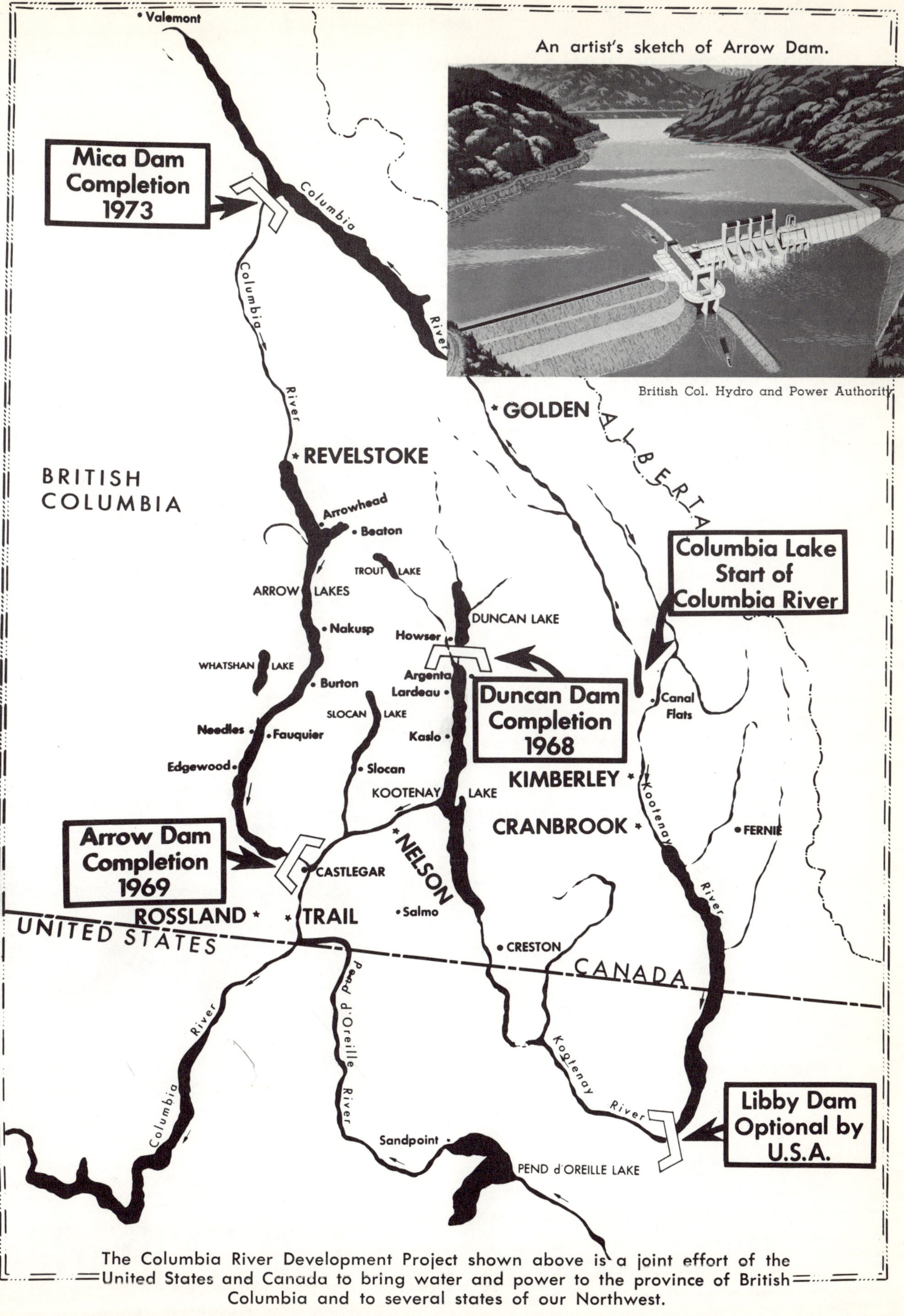

The Columbia River Development Project shown above is a joint effort of the United States and Canada to bring water and power to the province of British Columbia and to several states of our Northwest.

Conservation and Full Utilization

Prepared by U.S. DEPARTMENT OF THE INTERIOR · Bureau of Reclam

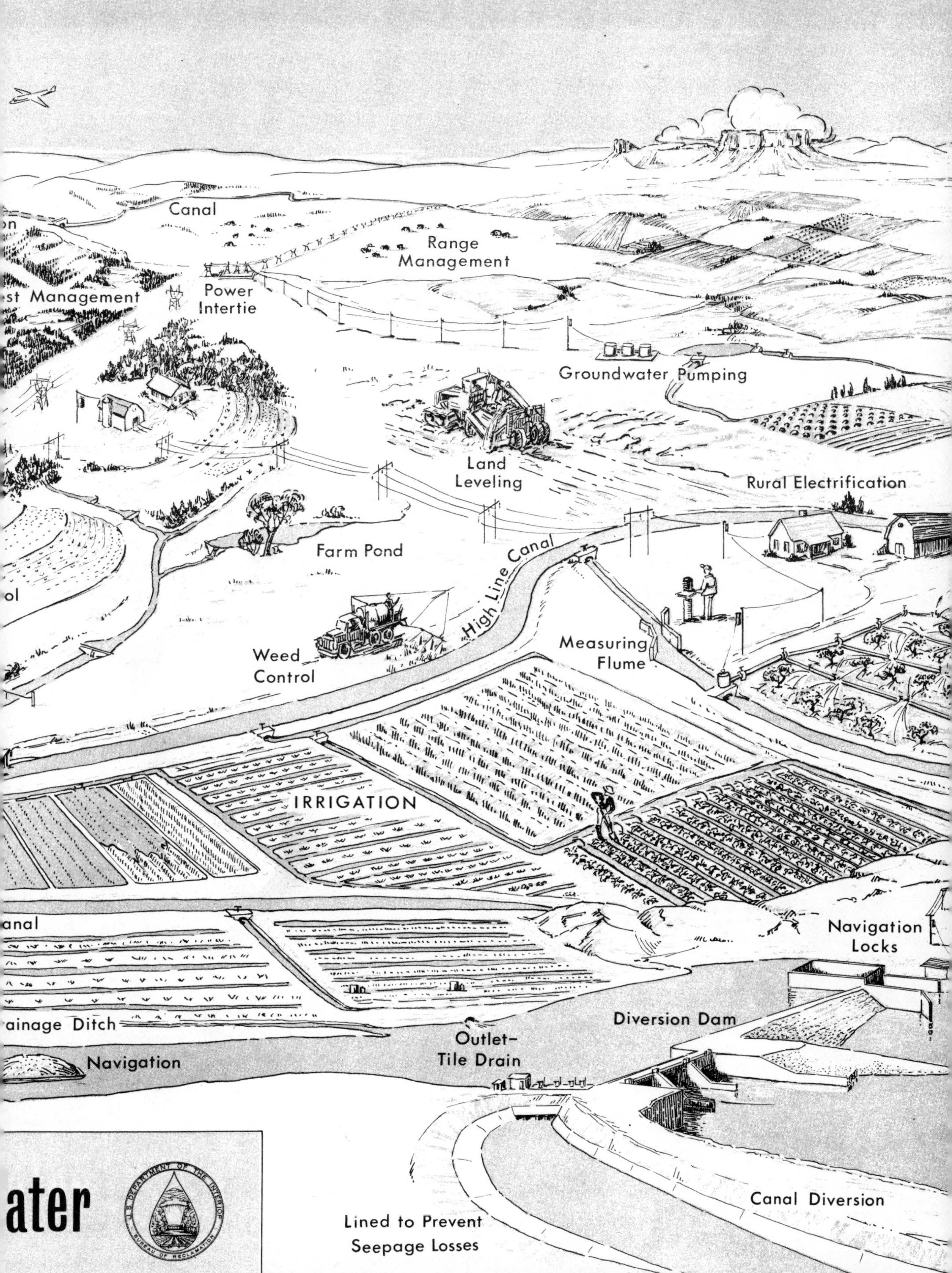

Canal
Range Management
Power Intertie
st Management
Groundwater Pumping
Land Leveling
Rural Electrification
Farm Pond
High Line Canal
Measuring Flume
ol
Weed Control
IRRIGATION
anal
Navigation Locks
ainage Ditch
Navigation
Outlet-Tile Drain
Diversion Dam
ater
U.S. DEPARTMENT OF THE INTERIOR
BUREAU OF RECLAMATION
Lined to Prevent Seepage Losses
Canal Diversion

Am. Museum of Natural History

NYC Parks Dept.

USDA

CHAPTER 4

LAND AND SOIL

"Land" and "soil" are terms we often use interchangeably. Conservationists, however, make a distinction between the two. Land is a broader term than soil. Soil is always land, for example, but land is not always soil. According to Webster's Dictionary, land is "the solid part of the surface of the earth." And soil is defined by the United States Department of Agriculture as "the natural medium for the growth of land plants."

There is not very much land, and there is even less soil. Of the earth's entire surface — 197 million square miles — only 29 per cent is land. This 57 million square miles includes vast areas in which no one can live — the frozen wastelands of Antarctica, inland waters such as the Great Lakes, and nine million square miles of barren desert.

Soil lies like a patchwork quilt across all land except steep, rugged mountain peaks and areas of perpetual ice and snow. It is soil that nourishes the crops that we eat, the cotton we weave into clothes, and the trees from which we cut wood for homes and furniture and paper. Civilization depends upon the cultivation of soil.

In 1798, an English economist, Thomas Malthus, predicted t h a t since the world's population tends to increase faster than the world's food supply, the excess population would die of starvation, disease, or violence. Malthus's prediction, fortunately, has not yet come to pass. That is because increased yields of crops and the use of new lands have enabled the supply of food to keep pace with the population growth. But there is still some danger that Malthus's grim prophecy may come true. Scientific advances in medicine and sanitation have increased the chances of life by reducing death rates in most countries and as a result, the world's population is increasing so rapidly that in 40 years it will double.

Even today, the people of countries like India and China live on the edge of famine. How will we feed twice as many people with substantially the same amount of soil? Our chief hope is to use our soil wisely. We must continue to increase crop yields, draw new and more food from the sea, and cultivate undeveloped land (deserts, for example); we must continue our research in developing concentrated food nutrients and in the soilless growth of plants; we must improve insect and pest control, and extend soil conservation practices.

We must also use our land prudently. Land provides minerals for fuels, metals for tools and machines — and space on which we and our domestic animals and wildlife can live. Until recently, we did not think of land as space, but today where three out of four Americans live in crowded urban areas, space is at a premium. We must plan for adequate space in our cities to take care of housing, parks, business and roads. The land in New York City's Central Park, for example, would command billions of dollars on the open market; but to the people of New York City it is priceless as a park.

A Profile Of Soil

Soil, the link between the earth's rock core and life, consists mainly of minerals, organic matter, water, and air in varying proportions. The proper combination of these elements makes soil good for growing crops. But not all soil is arable, that is, suitable for plant growth. Many desert soils are rich in minerals, organic matter and air; but they lack water and so they cannot be cultivated without special irrigation. Americans are fortunate in that more than half of the land in the United States is arable. Twenty per cent of this total is in cropland and 34 per cent is in forests. The rest is in pasture.

There are more than 70,000 kinds of soil in America, and they range from sand to clay to loam to muck to peat. Soil depth also varies from place to place. In some areas, it barely covers the rock, in others it may be hundreds or even thousands of feet thick. But, every soil, no mat-

USDA

Profile of poor soil, easily blown away.

ter how deep or shallow, has a soil profile. These are well-defined layers (horizons which vary in color, thickness, texture and structure.) You can see these solid horizons in excavations for buildings, highways, pipelines, or wherever steep cuts are made in the earth's surface.

The three principal soil horizons are topsoil, subsoil, and weathered rock. Topsoil is usually only a few inches thick. But it is a precious few inches because it contains more organic matter than the layers beneath it, and this makes it best for cultivation. It may take several million years to produce an inch of topsoil and, once gone, it cannot be replaced.

Topsoil is the layer that is most often abused by man. Five thousand years ago, for example, the Mediterranean island of Crete was the center of a prosperous civilization; today, the land's topsoil is gone, Crete is practically a barren rock, and its people are poverty-stricken.

Fertile soil profile with nearly two feet of top soil.

USDA

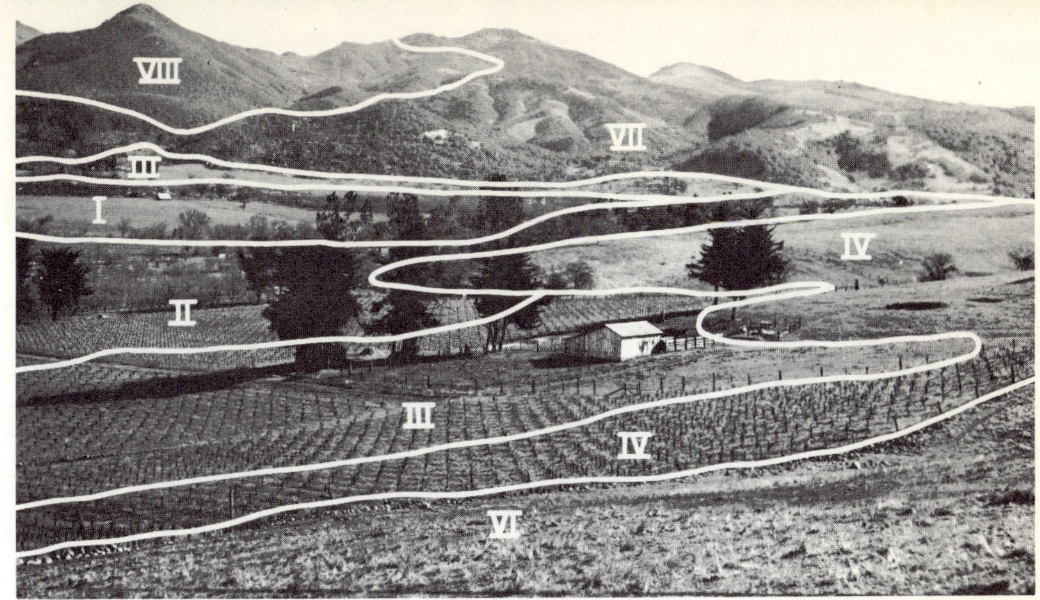

Classes of soil.

USDA

What happens to topsoil determines the fate of the second horizon, the subsoil. Some subsoils resemble, in texture and mineral content, the topsoil above them and crops sometimes can be grown on them. Subsoil is not as resistant to weather as the topsoil is, so once the topsoil is washed or blown away, the unprotected layer soon follows it. Only conservation practices can prevent this.

The t h i r d horizon, weathered rock, is as the name implies, a very rough soil. It has even less defense against the weather than subsoil, and crops will not grow there.

Although the United States has so much "agricultural" land, not all of it is suitable for cultivation. The Department of Agriculture divides our soils into eight classes. Soils in Classes I, II and III — lowland soils — may be continuously cultivated and used for many purposes. Class I and Class II soils, the best, have no special conservation problems, but Class III soils have problems of slope, soil depth, or drainage which limit their use and require various conservation practices to keep them productive. Soil conservation is most important with Class III soils.

Class IV soils are less productive and require more intensive conservation protection. Class V soils are good for grass; Classes VI and VII, usually high ground soils, are good for trees. Class VIII soils are unfit for cultivation but they are suitable for watersheds, wildlife habitat, and recreation.

When grass goes, soil goes.

USDA

Good soil brings an abundance at food stores.

USDA

Formation Of Soil

At first, there were only rock, intense heat, storms and volcanoes.

No one knows the exact age of the earth, but scientists estimate it to be from four and one-half to ten billion years old. For many millions of years, nothing lived on the earth. There were no plants, no animals, just a mass of volcanoes, rock, and water. From the beginning, however, the earth's surface constantly changed; it is still changing. Weathering — the destructive action of water, ice, heat, cold, and wind on rock — was the first physical action to affect the earth's surface. Weathering reduces solid rock to particles. It is a long, slow, and continuous process, speeded up only by violent upheavals of the earth's surface, such as earthquakes and volcanic eruptions.

But, the destructive weathering of rock is not enough to produce soil. Another process, a constructive process, that of biological action is necessary. The first biological action was that of plants. Millions of years ago, primitive plants appeared in the sea. Eventually, after many changes in form, they made their way to land. Algae were the first, later they were followed by the mosses. Ferns succeeded the mosses, and so on. As they lived and died and decayed, these plants added organic matter to the fine, weathered rock particles. Later, higher plant life began to grow and added more organic matter to produce richer soils. Still later, animals developed and fed on plants and made their organic contributions to the soil. Thus, through long, slow eons of weathering and biological action, a layer of soil formed over part of the earth's original rocky surface.

As soil contributes food to plants and animals, so do plants and animals contribute food to soil. Plants take their nourishment from the soil and the air, and when they die they fall on soil and are eaten and their remains are broken down by earthworms, animals, and bacteria. The more this happens, the better the soil. Some of the best pasture land contains 3,000 pounds of earthworms per acre. This is more than the weight of the animals that graze on that much land!

So, plants and animals depend upon soil and soil depends upon plants and animals. This is an important principle in planning ways of conserving soil and making it productive.

Travelers Insurance Co.

Early man lived on animals nourished by sparse soil.

USDA

Plants, animals, water and sunlight keep soil in balance.

Erosion, The Greatest Enemy Of The Soil

USDA

Erosion is a normal and continuous process in which natural forces, such as water, wind, and frost, cause soil and rock to be worn away from the land. It is a slow process — except when man's careless use of the land speeds it up. For example, it took millions of years to wear down the Appalachian Mountains whose rounded hills once were sharply peaked like the Rockies, but it has only taken a few years to lose the fertile topsoil of the "Dust Bowl" regions of Texas, Oklahoma, and Kansas.

The principal agents of erosion are water and wind. Water evaporates from the sea and land and returns as rain or snow. It falls first on topsoil. If the soil is well covered with plants, or if it has been protected through good conservation practices, the water either sinks into the ground or moves slowly down-

hill, and erosion is avoided. But, if improper farming have left the land and slopes exposed, the falling rain will form a sheet of water and run downhill, carrying the finer particles of soil with it. This is called sheet erosion.

Little streams often form as the amount of runoff water increases. These streams wash the soil away and leave little rills, which may be several inches deep. This is called rill erosion. The rills often join to form larger, deeper channels or gullies. Deep gullies are almost impossible to repair through normal cultivation. Gullies may become severe enough to make farm or rangeland useless. The streams deposit eroded soil on rich bottomlands where it is not needed, carry silt to clog reservoirs, and deepen channels by removing moisture quickly after a rain. Gullies reduce the amount of water

Tennessee Valley Authority and U.S. Forest Service

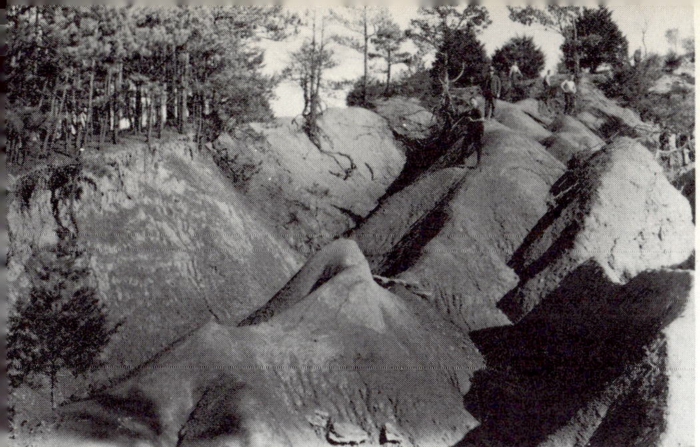

Eroded forest land.

Tennessee Valley Authority and U.S. Forest Service

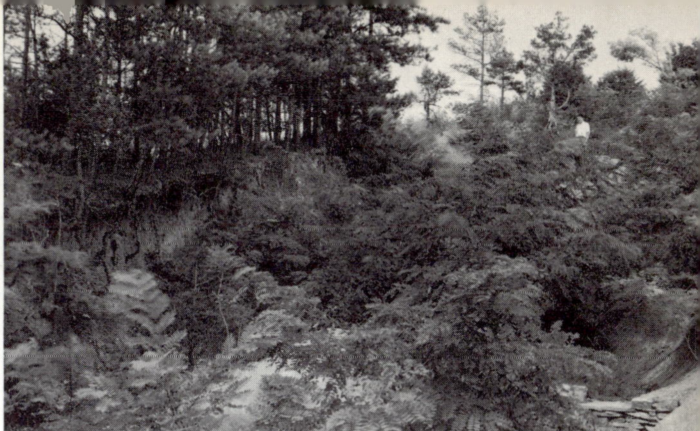

The same eroded area after reclamation.

available for crops and may even lower the water table because the rain water has no opportunity to sink into the ground to replenish underground aquifers. Silt from gully erosion also may damage roads, railroads, streets, and sewer systems.

Flat land, if it is not properly managed, also may be damaged by water. Rain may pack the soil so hard that it cannot absorb water, which then evaporates before it can provide the moisture that is essential for growing crops.

Wind erodes dry soils that are unprotected by vegetation. Land that is open to wind erosion may be perfectly flat, rolling, or hilly but wind erosion is most common in flat lands of moderate rainfall. Wind picks up soil particles from the dry, unprotected soil and moves them to new locations where, like silt from water erosion, they are neither wanted nor needed. Dust storms are the most obvious examples of wind erosion. Silt from wind erosion then covers highways, fields, pastures, and airport runways. It seeps into homes and stores. But, worst of all, it leaves bare the land from which it was swept.

USDA

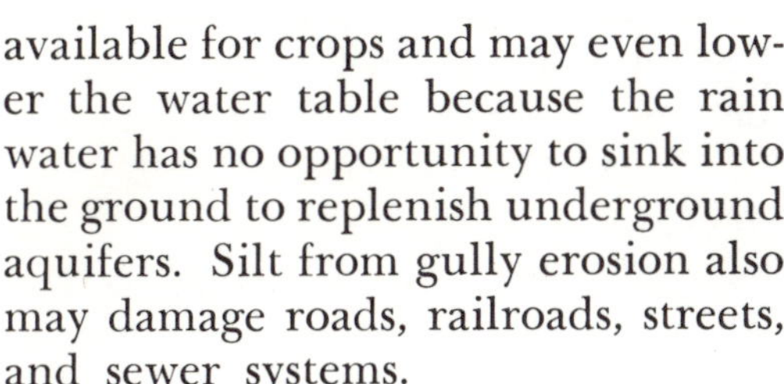

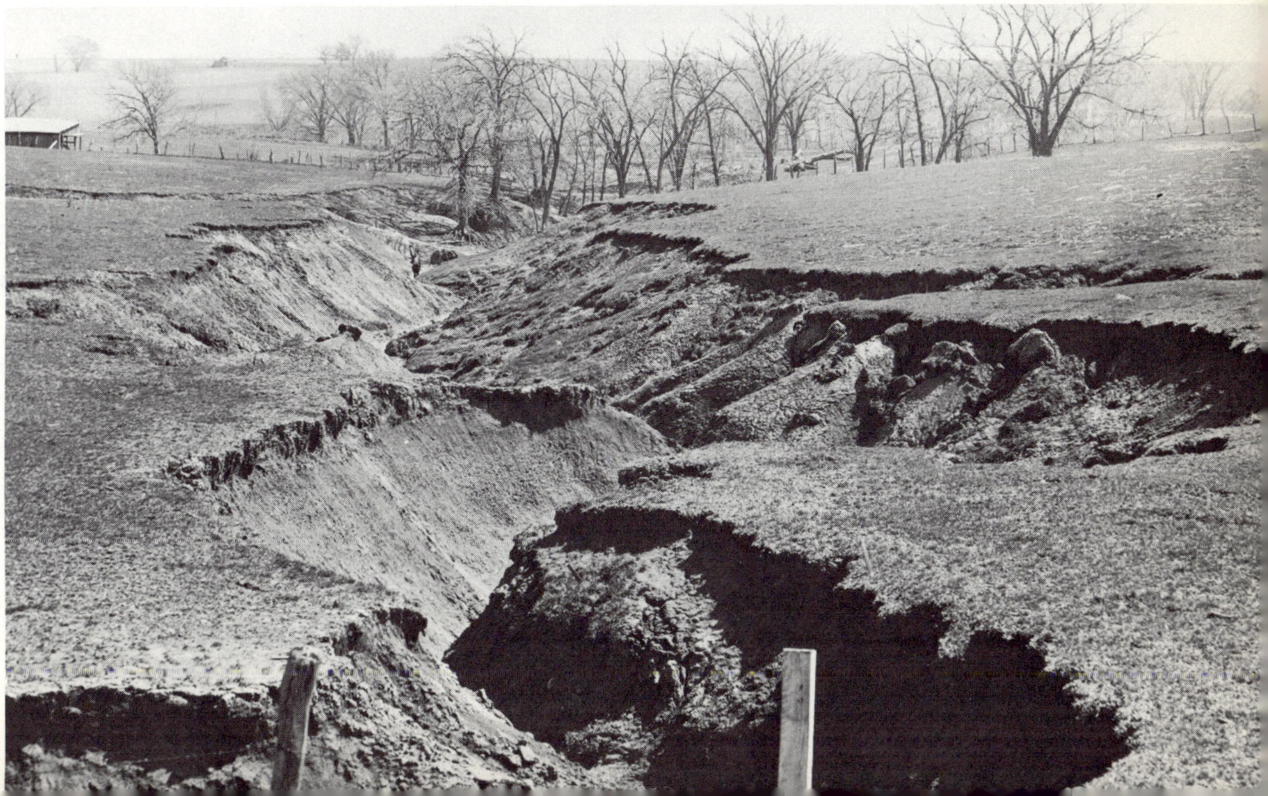

Signs Of Erosion

Erosion often goes unnoticed because it usually leaves some soil on the land. Also, if erosion wears away the soil of an area evenly, as sheet erosion does, it may take an expert to spot the damage. But, there are certain unmistakable signs of erosion that anyone can see. You probably can find some the next time you are in the country or park area.

Rills and gullies, of course, indicate soil erosion. Muddy water is another proof. Its color is caused by silt in runoff water from unprotected land during a heavy rain. Ditches, streams, and rivers become brown or even red as their silt loads increase. After drying up, even small mud puddles on or below eroded land contain a layer of silt.

Stony fields are often the result of sheet erosion which has washed away fine soil, thus exposing stones or gravel. Where stony soils are poorly drained, stones are sometimes forced to the surface by frost which heaves the soil upward.

Exposed tree roots are proof of erosion that has removed the soil above them because tree roots naturally grow under the soil. Bare spots on pastures or grazing land are signs of soil erosion. Too many animals feed on the grass and pack the land hard with their movements. This also can

USDA

Soil piling up against a farmhouse.

Three feet of topsoil piled against the hedge after a rain.

USDA

USDA

Home owners need to prevent erosion, too.

Streambank erosion, in which good soil is being washed into the stream — destroying its value as soil and muddying the stream for fish and vegetation.

Streambank cutting is a spectacular form of erosion. Strong currents, ice and debris in swollen streams cut away the soil on the banks, and carry it downstream to clog reservoirs and cover farmlands and highways. Fields or even whole farms may be cut in two by bank erosion severe enough to change the stream channel. Sometimes ponds and small reservoirs become completely filled with silt from nearby eroded fields.

Rivers, harbors, and large reservoirs also suffer from erosion to such an extent that continuous dredging is necessary to keep them useful. Dredging in canals, harbors, and large reservoirs is proof of serious erosion in the watersheds that provide their water. The Mississippi Delta below New Orleans, about 13,000 square miles of rich land, is composed of silt brought down by the great river from eroded lands all along its course.

happen in parks, where too many people might trample the ground hard. Since water cannot percolate into this hard soil, it removes the better soil in spots, exposing the poorer soil beneath. On many higher sloping lands, topsoil has been eroded away to expose the lighter-colored sub-quality soils. Meanwhile, the eroded topsoil may have settled on lower fields, where, since it appears darker than the surrounding soil, it can be seen from a nearby hill or from an airplane.

Stone walls, hedges, and fences are good measures of protection against erosion on a slope. Runoff water, slowed down by these barriers, may deposit as much as three feet of silt above them. The difference in elevations above and below these barriers indicate how much soil has been eroded. Look for such signs of erosion in the suburbs and along the land bordering highways.

A water supply source filled with silt from soil runoff.

Lessons From History

Agriculture got its start more than 7,000 years ago in fertile river valleys. It has been plagued by erosion ever since.

In ancient Mesopotamia, farmers produced food crops by irrigating their dry plains land with the muddy waters of the Tigris and Euphrates Rivers. The mud in these rivers was silt that had been washed down from higher, eroded land, and as Mesopotamia's population increased and irrigation canals were extended from the rivers, this silt clogged up the canals. For many years, laborers (often prisoners of war) dredged the silt out of the canals and kept them open. But, the task was too great even for a country of 20 million people. The canals became so choked with silt that they could no longer deliver water to farmlands, and villages and cities eventually disappeared.

Some people, on the other hand, have overcome great handicaps by

Am. Museum of Natural History

The Incas built terraces on steep mountain slopes 1,000 years ago to prevent runoff.

practicing conservation methods on the land. The ancient Incas grew potatoes and maize high in the Andes Mountains by terracing the steep land. The Japanese, on the other side of the world, used the same method to grow rice whose cultivation has gone on for many hundreds of years. The Israelis have irrigated millions of acres of desert and planted crops where before there were only swamps.

The Nile River at flood time.   Am. Museum of Natural History

Growing rice on terraces in use after 3,000 years of farming, Japan.

Profile of rice-growing area, Philippine Islands. Almost two-thirds of the world's population, depend on rice for survival. For them, soil conservation is a matter of life or death.

The history of soil conservation in America is unsatisfactory. When the first colonists came to America, its soils were fertile and well protected by forests and vast, lush fields of grass. The rivers were clear and fast-flowing. Then the settlers cut down the forests to clear land for crops and extensively farmed the grassy plains. Their farming methods were so careless that after only 300 years, more than two-thirds of the farm land eroded faster than new soil could be formed. In the 1930's, a vast area of plains land turned into a "Dust Bowl." In some states, unused but plowed land on a moderate slope now loses 29 per cent of the rainfall and 64 tons of soil per acre each year. In other states, on land continuously cultivated with only one crop, 10 per cent of the annual rainfall and 22 tons of soil per acre are lost each year. At this rate, it would take only 44 years to lose seven inches of soil. If crops were scientifically rotated on this same land it would take 109 years to lose that much soil from erosion. And, if the land were kept in grass, rainfall loss would be only one per cent, and so little soil would be washed away that it would take 96,000 years to lose only seven inches.

We have learned the same bitter lesson from the destruction of our great forests. Where forests are completely protected from fire, soil loss is so slight that the formation of new soil far exceeds loss from erosion. In fact, in a protected forest only seven inches of soil would be lost in a half-million years — but more than that would be formed to balance the loss.

Conservation Is Everyone's Responsibility

Three-fourths of America's land area is privately owned and 60 per cent of this land is in farms and ranches. Since farmers and ranchers also use some of the public lands, — such as the National Forests and Grasslands and the part of the public domain allotted to grazing — they influence the use and care of soil, water, trees, shrubs, and wildlife of about 85 per cent of the nation's land area. The greatest task in soil erosion control is extending conservation practices to privately-owned land.

Much forest land has been cleared for farms, although its soil is unsuitable for growing crops or even for pasture. The best practice for such land would be to reforest it and plant trees. If conservation is to be successful on all private land (as it already is on much of it), the owner of the land must act according to the land's particular needs and problems. His first step is to prepare a survey which shows the type and conditions of his land. The owner of range or grassland, for example, must know how many head of livestock can graze on his land without damaging it.

Most landowners, unable to prepare such a plan themselves, become cooperators in their local Soil Conservation District. These districts include about 98 per cent of the farms and ranches, and 94 per cent of all the agricultural land in the United States. They are independent units of the state governments, not agencies of the federal government. The Soil Conservation Service of the United States Department of Agri-

USDA

A conservation technician advises a Delaware farmer participating in the soil conservation district.

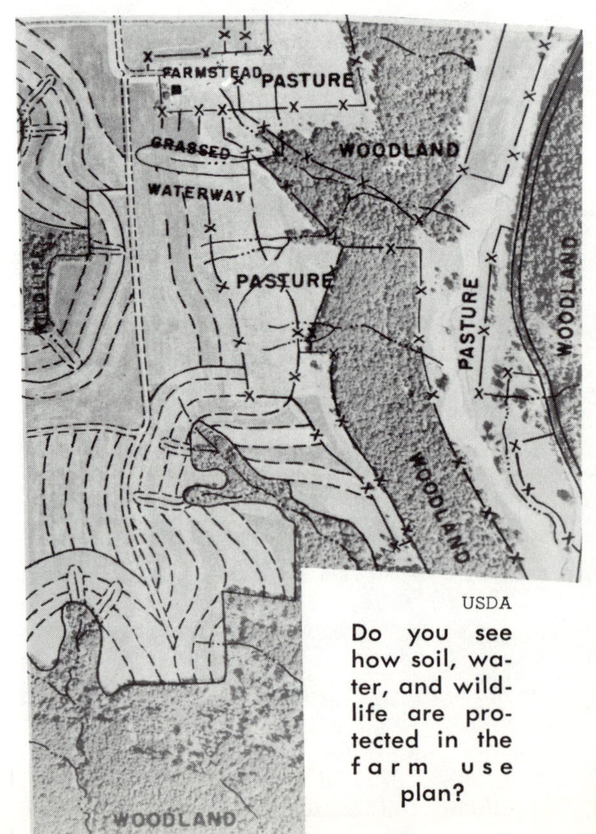

USDA

Do you see how soil, water, and wildlife are protected in the farm use plan?

Windbreaks (left to right) of ash, American Elm, and, lilac to protect the barley crop against erosion.

Ground cover must be planted at once along a roadside if erosion is to be prevented.

culture, however, provides technical assistance to the districts and to individual cooperating landowners. Soil conservation technicians will make a free survey of an owner's land and recommend what the land is best suited for and what conservation practices are best for it. Then the landowner decides what action he is willing to take. If erosion is present in any form, his first step will be to stop that erosion and prevent any more. Irrigation to grow crops or improve pastures may be a necessary part of soil conservation.

Some conservation measures are best applied when several landowners cooperate in a single program. The farmers in a watershed area, for example, may join together to take major soil conservation and flood prevention measures which would be too costly for an individual farmer. It may be necessary to build a large reservoir to collect water during violent storms. This type of reservoir lets the water out slowly to prevent a flood further downstream. Sometimes, through careful planning, reservoirs are made large enough to store extra water for urban and industrial use and for recreation.

Conservation practices may also be applied to urban soils. Some soils are not suitable for the construction of houses — the foundations may slide or the land may become easily flooded. These soils can be used as small parks or other spots of beauty scattered throughout a city. In this way, we not only conserve the soil, but we improve the city as well.

Future farmers of Hawaii.

Soil Conservation On The Farm

USDA

Where once a good wheat crop grew, Maryland.

USDA

Terracing protects the corn and the soil, Illinois.

Bitter experience has taught us much about soil conservation. Sometimes the best we can do is to repair old damage. For example, we know that cropland so badly damaged by gullies that it can no longer be farmed should be fenced to keep out grazing animals. Then, perhaps, it can be planted to trees or grass, which will stabilize the soil, prevent further erosion, and cover the scars of the past.

But there are ways to prevent erosion from starting. One way is by contour plowing, that is, plowing along the contour of the land, around the hills instead of straight up and down. This slows down the movement of rain water and allows the previous moisture to sink into the ground instead of carrying off soil.

Strip-cropping is another conservation practice. Crops are planted in strips in which every other strip is planted to grasses that have plenty of leaves and roots — wheat, oats, or barley. The alternating strips are row crops such as corn or cotton. Contour, strip-cropping or a combination of the two are the first steps in erosion control and water conservation.

Sometimes sloping land must be terraced to catch rain water and direct it into outlets such as grassed waterways. The terraces, long ridges of soil, are built on the contour of the land. They form gently sloping ditches to carry away excess water. Crops between the terraces are also arranged on the contour. On sloping ground, not only annual crops but perennial crops — such as orchards

A prosperous farm in Wisconsin.

Looking over a job well done, Maryland.

— are planted on the contour, with terraces between them.

Farms in the Northeast frequently contain good soil on slopes that are too steep for crop cultivation. To cultivate the land on these steep hills would expose it to erosion, so the land is kept in grass and used as pasture for dairy cows. This is good sense and good conservation policy.

Farm ponds are frequently necessary to catch and hold water for livestock, irrigation, and fire prevention. Farmers are building about 60,000 of them a year. Many ponds are converted gullies or abandoned quarries, others are dug out of open fields. They are evidence of good soil conservation and incidentally, many of these ponds become good areas for fishing, boating, and swimming.

Where wind is a hazardous element and causes more erosion than water, as in the American Southwest, windbreaks of several rows of trees are planted in the path of the wind. Windbreaks force the wind upward and slow its movement across the fields beyond the trees. The slower moving air does not blow soil away. Much of the land itself is planted in crops with plenty of leaves and roots to help hold the soil in place.

These conservation practices, which are common in the United States, also are being used by farmers in Australia, Egypt, India, Brazil, Mexico, Canada and newly-developed nations of Africa and Asia through technical assistance from the Food and Agriculture Organization of the United Nations.

Soil Conservation On The Range

Good pasture, good breeding, good conservation add up to good beef.

There are 950 million acres of rangeland in the United States, 725 million in the western states (the Western Range) and the remaining 225 million acres are in the Midwest, the Southwest, and the South. The dividing line between the two broad range areas is at about 100° Meridian, slightly west of Fort Worth, Texas.

On rangeland grow native plants, called forage, which are suitable for feeding livestock, such as cattle, sheep, and horses. It is different from intensively-managed, improved pasture where, through the use of seed, fertilizers, cultivation and even irrigation, new and improved forage plants can be grown. Rangeland, particularly the Western Range, has its own conservation problems.

On many large areas of rangeland, particularly in the West, overgrazing has caused soil and plant damage. More animals were allowed to graze on the land than there was food to support them, or grazing was allowed too early in the spring before

Denuded land from overgrazing, Nez-perce National Forest, Idaho.

the soil and plants were ready. Over-grazing so badly damaged this soil that it no longer produces enough forage to feed livestock, and it is doubtful that even intensive soil conservation practices could restore its forage production capacity.

There are three classes of over-grazed rangeland: fair, poor and very poor. On a fair range, good forage plants have been reduced in number and their place taken by weeds, poorer grasses or shrubs. Plant cover and litter are less than on a good range. Reduced organic matter in the topsoil has lessened its capacity to hold moisture, and the resulting runoff water is heavy with silt. With good soil conservation methods, fair rangeland can be restored; without them, it soon becomes poor range-land.

Poor rangeland produces only a small fraction of the forage that would grow on good land. Low-value annual plants, weeds, and shrubs are most of the vegetative cover. Much topsoil has been eroded away, exposing the subsoil; and since there is little organic matter left in the soil and its waterholding capacity is low, runoff is fast. There is both sheet and rill erosion. Rebuilding a poor range is a major soil conservation task that may take decades and cost more money than the average land owner can afford.

Very poor rangeland has an extremely low grazing capacity and only a thin cover of low-value plants, m o s t l y annuals or unpalatable shrubs. There is practically no top-soil. Erosion is severe, with extensive gullies. Summer storms, because of the soil's low water-holding capacity, cause flash floods. Generally, it is impractical to reclaim very poor rangeland for grazing purposes. The conservation measures needed would be so costly that only the need for critical watershed protection would justify their use.

Overgrazed pasture on poor land, Texas.

Progress In Soil Conservation

Strange as it may seem, conservation of the soil has only recently become a national policy. Forest and wildlife conservation date back to the early 1900's, but soil conservation did not begin until 1933, when there was a great crisis resulting from a series of severe dust storms in the Southwest and Midwest. A small soil conservation agency was established in the United States Department of the Interior. Nothing much happened until 1935, when Congress established the Soil Conservation Service in the Department of Agriculture.

The Service is one of the most efficient, aggressive, and successful of all federal agencies. It has been particularly successful in overcoming the fears of over-regulation and domination held by many private landowners and businessmen. Today, business corporations, banks, farm and construction equipment manufacturers, state and local governments, civic organizations, as well as individual farmers and ranchers work willingly for soil conservation programs and wise resource management.

From the beginning, the Soil Conservation Service recognized that soil and water conservation could not be separated. That is why the Watershed Protection and Flood Prevention Act was needed. This Act allows the U. S. Department of Agriculture, through the Soil Conservation Service, to help local organizations plan watershed protection and flood prevention on small watersheds of 250,000 acres or less. The Agriculture Department provides technical assistance, cost-sharing, and credit to the local watershed project.

If you could have flown back and forth across the country in the 1920's, you would have seen dramatically how man had abused the land. You would have passed patches of barren fields, stretches of burned-out forests, and dry, dusty plains. Today, on the same trip, you can see the benefits of soil management — a colorful patch-quilt pattern of rich cropland, lush forests, and green grasslands.

If you drive through the countryside, you will see that even highways and roads which once were built haphazardly, are planned to enhance the scenic views while they help prevent erosion through plantings. The impression is one of abundance and plenty, of beauty and practical usefulness. Yet, much still remains to be done, not only in the open areas of field and forest, but also in the cities and sprawling suburbs. The same planning and scientific research that have been successful in rural America now need to be applied to urban America.

Urban planners should work with conservationists to plan green spots and to construct buildings so that they do not shut out air and light. Trees and neighborhood parks should be expanded. Transportation should be planned to make the best use of vital land and to beautify the areas built as highways. When people of the crowded cities can walk or cycle to a quiet open area — be it grassy or woodland — they will have the best of everything, the rich variety of city living blended with the quiet mood of the open country.

Dust storms, 1935.

USDA

USDA

City planners work with rural conservationists,
Stamford, Connecticut.

USDA

America the beautiful.

Hydrologists study soil runoff.

USDA

City boys learn about soil, New Jersey.

USDA

U.S. Forest Service   Vitagraph, Inc.

CHAPTER 5

FORESTS

Early America was built from wood. Cabins, fences, bridges, barns, furniture, riverboats, wagons, stockades, railroad ties — all were hewn from the lush forests that blanketed much of the continent. Today, our forests still are one of our most valuable resources. They are the source of more than 5,000 products, including pulp for paper and lumber for building. Forests protect our land, our watersheds, and our wildlife. They give us beauty, majesty, and woodland retreats for recreation and the study of living things.

All these benefits, and many more, come from our forests. But many people do not realize this; they think of forests mainly as a source of wood. Like the early colonists who had to cut the trees to clear fields for crops, they say, "Cut them down and saw them up."

About 1900, we began to consider the idea that timber should be cultivated and harvested as a crop, not "mined" indiscriminately. Until that time we had been slashing our forests to make way for new farms and roads, to extend railroad lines, to build new homes, towns and cities, to supply our growing industries, and to provide timber.

In 1905, President Theodore Roosevelt established the Forest Service in the United States Department of Agriculture. Gifford Pinchot, the first great conservationist, became its first chief. National forest reserves were set aside to protect watersheds and supply timber; additional national parks were established; owners of forest lands were encouraged to treat forests as crops that needed management and fire protection for continual yield. The Forest Service encouraged research in the control of pests and disease as enemies of trees. Forests began to be recognized for their value in protecting soil and watersheds, and the cooperation of local and state agencies was developed.

Today, our forests are in better shape than they were 50 years ago, thanks to conservation methods employed by both industry and government. One-third of the United States is still covered by forests, mostly in the East and Northwest. But our timber needs are great and are increasing very rapidly. It is estimated that to meet the needs of population growth, expanded chemical use of wood, and the tremendous rise in paper consumption, we will need to double forest growth by the year 2000. Can this be done? We already have the necessary land, knowledge, and techniques for conserving our forests; to put these into widespread practice will require better communication and education. We need to "overcome the inertia of the unconcerned," as one expert recently expressed it.

How Trees Grow

The forest is a community of many kinds of plants and animals. Every living thing in the forest — every tree, plant, bird, reptile, insect, mammal — helps to keep the community in balance. Shrews and moles, though seldom seen, plow and aerate soil to make it more absorbent to water and air. The soil produces plants whose roots hold the topsoil together, prevent erosion, and provide channels for water to penetrate into the ground. Plant tissue becomes food for insects, animals, and birds. These decompose after they die and help fertilize the soil. The natural cycle of life and death in the forest continues day after day, week after week, month after month, year after year.

Each tree struggles upward toward the light needed for the leaves to produce food. The hardier trees grow tall and their leaves form the forest canopy. Lower branches, lacking light, die, and drop off. The tree develops a long, branchless trunk with a narrow crown of leaves high above the ground. This type of narrow tree growth produces the best

U.S. Forest Service

lumber. Trees that grow in the open, where there is space in which to expand outward, develop short trunks and wide-spreading branches. They are good for shade, but they produce a poor grade of lumber.

Trees grow either from seeds or from sprouts. Many seeds must be produced for a few to grow since so few survive. To germinate, seeds must fall where they can get moisture, light, and warmth. As soon as the roots penetrate the earth, they

U.S. Forest Service

pick up mineral nutrients and moisture from the soil and carry them upward through the main stems to the leaves. In the tiny cells of green leaves, the tree produces its own food through the chemical process of photosynthesis. Chlorophyll, the green substance of leaves, captures the light and energy of the sun, combines them with carbon dioxide from the air, and the water and nutrients from the soil to produce a simple sugar. This sugar is later changed into another simple food and then to wood.

Each year a layer of new wood cells is formed between the outside layer and the bark. This is visible as a "growth ring." If the rings are counted accurately, they show the age and history of the tree. By the regularity or irregularity, rings reveal a disease or when fire may have attacked the growing tree.

Buds grow on the twigs of the tree. Within each scale-covered bud lies the beginning of next year's flowers and leaves. The flowers of mature trees give off pollen grains and, when pollination takes place, seeds form. In the oak tree the seeds are the acorns.

A tree, like a person, can grow old. It slows down its growth, as revealed by narrowing annual rings; leaves often grow smaller, some branches die and wither, insects or disease attack it, and, finally, the tree dies.

There are several distinct elements in a tree. Wood cellulose makes up almost half of its bulk. These are the fibers from which paper and paper products are produced. Cellu-lose also is an important chemical agent in the manufacture of rayon, rubber, explosives, waxes, soaps, fishing lures, ice cream, and toothpaste.

The wood cellulose fibers are held together by lignin, the sticky substance that binds the tree fibers. Lignin is used as a binder in road building, oil drilling, and in the production of insecticides, dyes, and mineral tonics. Researchers are working on new ways to use this valuable chemical. They believe that lignin — the discarded substance in papermaking — eventually will prove to be as useful as cellulose.

Many useful medicines are obtained from cascara bark, ginseng root, quinine, storax gum, witch hazel bark, wild cherry bark, and mandrake. The sap and gum are used for maple sugar, resins, and turpentine.

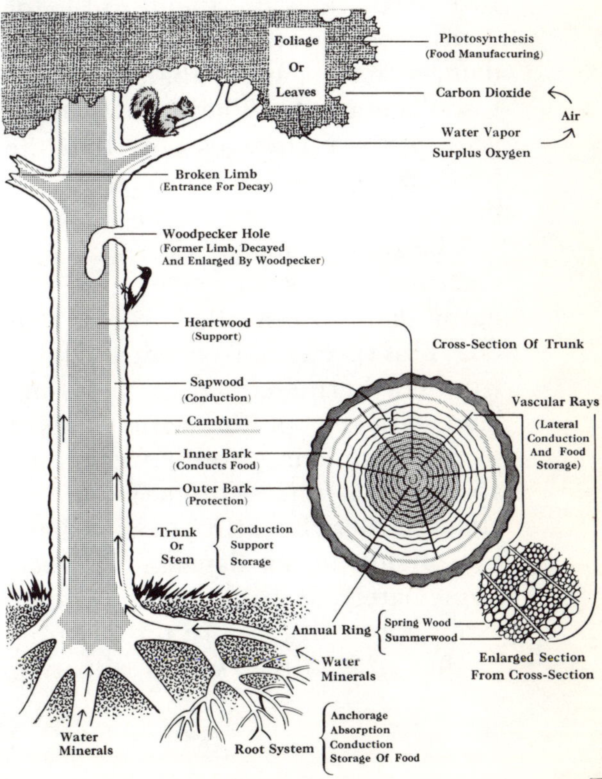

Tree Disease

U.S. Forest Service

White pine blister rust.

Diseases caused by fungi kill some trees, stunt the growth of many more, and destroy the heartwood in mature trees, making them unfit for many wood products. Tree diseases damage forests more than all other forest enemies. They slow forest growth to a large extent, but the total damage is not as great as the damage done by insects or weather.

The destruction of the American chestnut tree is an example of the harm that uncontrolled disease can do. This species of tree, with a range from northern Georgia to New England, was one of the nation's most prized commercial forest trees until about 1900. Then a blight from Asia attacked these beautiful trees. Chestnut blight did not damage the wood immediately, as would so many other forms of tree disease. In the chestnut blight, the tiny spores floating through the air settled on the bark of healthy trees, grew through the surface, and eventually killed the trees.

Within a few years, the blight had killed practically every American chestnut tree in the United States. Many dead trees can still be seen along the Skyline Drive in Virginia and North Carolina where white tree skeletons remain as monuments to a disease that has never been controlled. There is still some hope. Scientists have found a few living American chestnut trees that are resistant to the disease. They hope that from these trees a disease-resistant strain of the American chestnut will be developed, and this beautiful and useful tree may once again become part of our forest.

Another disease, white pine blister rust, kills five-needled pines in all parts of the country, mainly the white pines of the East and West and the sugar pines of California and southern Oregon. Blister rust was introduced into the United States about 1910 through nursery seedlings imported from Europe. Strangely enough, pines can be protected from this disease merely by destroying currant and gooseberry bushes. Scientists found through careful study that the disease enters the pine through the needles and moves into the bark, causing bark cankers. About three years later, these cankers form blisters which release millions of spores that are scattered by wind for many miles. The spores cannot infect the pine; instead they attack the leaves of currant and gooseberry bushes.

The fungus grows on the bushes and forms brownish-yellow spots. The spots produce other spores that can infect pines, but these are short-lived and can spread for only a few hundred yards. So, in order to control blister rust, foresters remove the currant and gooseberry plants from areas surrounding a stand of pine trees. Another control against the disease is to plant a type of pine tree that seems to be resistant or immune to the disease.

Another enemy of trees is the Dutch elm disease which came from Europe on elm logs in the 1930's. It threatens every American elm in the country and has already killed millions of these fine trees. No practical means of control has yet been found, but studies have shown that fewer healthy trees are infected if diseased trees are cut and burned as soon as they show signs of infection. This method of limiting the spread of the disease is more effective than spraying all elms with chemicals. It is also more humane, for the chemicals have been found to kill birds, especially robins.

The Dutch elm disease is carried from one elm to another by small bark beetles. If scientists find out how to control this beetle — without also endangering birds and other animals — they may be able to check the disease.

There are tree diseases that do not kill trees outright, but they damage the healthy wood and render the tree susceptible to infection. Such a disease is heart rot fungi, whose spores enter trees through wounds caused by broken branches, forest fires, or damaged bark and roots. Trees damaged by ice and wind are readily attacked by heart rot.

Foresters have learned to harvest storm-damaged trees, particularly the hardwoods, before heart rot gets a firm hold on them. Early removal of damaged trees is good forestry practice because it salvages timber before disease destroys it.

U.S. Forest Service

Asiatic chestnut blight caused by a fungus.

Defending Trees Against Insects

Each year, insects kill more trees than do forest fires or any other enemy of the forest. Their most serious attacks often follow forest fires or severe windstorms by which trees are weakened. Coniferous or evergreen forests are more susceptible to insect attack than are the deciduous trees.

Bark beetles are the deadliest enemy of coniferous trees. They dig tunnels under the bark and cut the food supply line between the leaves and roots. If these tunnels fully circle the tree, it dies. Bark beetles have caused great damage among the Douglas fir and the Engelmann spruce trees in the West and among evergreen forests in other parts of the country.

The spruce budworm, another destructive insect, eats leaves. It has caused heavy forest damage in fir and spruce forests in the Northeast, the Rocky Mountains, and the Pacific Northwest. This insect can completely defoliate a spruce or fir tree in a very short time, sometimes in hours.

Other forest insects deform the branches and tops of trees or bore into their trunks, reducing wood quality and decreasing the vitality of the tree by sucking its sap. Insects that feed on leaves, such as the spruce budworm, can be controlled by spraying infested forests from airplanes with chemicals. This has its hazards, however. Unless it is done with extreme care and in a solution that is safe for fish, birds, and other animals, chemical sprays can cause damage to wildlife and perhaps even to human beings that may be greater than the value of timber saved and watersheds protected.

Healthy, vigorous stands of trees usually are less susceptible to insect attack. Foresters, therefore, are always on the alert for insect outbreaks and remove infested trees before the insects do much damage. Since bark beetles cannot be controlled by airplane spraying, trees are protected by treatment with bark-penetrating insecticides. This is a monumental job, requiring heavy expenditures for labor, equipment, and chemicals.

Laboratory research to control insect damage to trees never ceases. The forest products industry, the states, and the United States Forest Service cooperate in a pest control program that may save many of our trees from insect destruction. Precautions are also taken to prevent diseased plants and animals from being brought in by travelers or cargoes. With increasing travel and trade among nations, plant inspection becomes especially important.

Engelmann spruce bark beetle larvae at work.

A forest fire
out of control.

Am. Forest Products Industries

Fire is the most dramatic and spectacular enemy of forests. Each year there are about 100,000 fires in the United States, causing damage to as many as five million acres of forest land.

The sad thing about forest fires is that nine out of ten are caused by people who are either careless or indifferent. The tenth fire is started accidentally by lightning, a power line break, or other accident. Many fires are deliberately set by "fire bugs" or incendiarists who, for some strange reason, like to see a forest in flames.

Careless campers, smokers, and trash burners are the chief causes of forest fires. They either build fires in the wrong places or do not put them out — dead out — before leaving. Spring and fall are the most hazardous times of the year for forest fires. Unless there are regular winter rains, the forest floor dries out quickly in the spring. If fires occur before the growing plants take over, they spread readily. Spring is a popular time of year for fishermen who often have careless smoking habits. In the fall, hunters may start fires when they drop lighted cigarettes over dried leaves and plants.

An intensive program of fire prevention education was started in 1941, when national defense in wartime made it necessary. War themes dominated the first fire prevention posters until 1944 when Bambi, a Walt Disney deer, appeared on posters. Bambi was very successful in appealing to people to prevent forest fires. But, in 1945, a new creature of the forest was introduced. He is Smokey Bear, a symbol of good forest manners. Smokey has made people alert to the dangers of fire in the woods.

The number of forest fires has dropped from 250,000 in 1941 to about 100,000 today, even though more Americans than ever make use of our forests. The Smokey Bear theme is the world's greatest success story in forest conservation. It has saved many lives and billions of dollars in timber, recreation areas, watershed, and soil damage. Smokey is supported by American industry and business, the states, the United States Forest Service and other public agencies, and the people.

Am. Forest Products Industries

A crown fire.

There are two main types of forest fires. "Crown" fires get into the tree tops as a result of high winds and travel rapidly through the forest, destroying trees, killing game and destroying wildlife habitat, burning buildings, and sometimes taking human lives. The most spectacular crown fires occur in coniferous forests of the West.

"Surface" fires are confined to the ground. They do not reach the tops of the trees and do not often kill larger trees. They are, however, very harmful since they scorch the bases of the big trees and open up wounds through which diseases may enter. Trees damaged by fire are vulnerable to insects, which frequently follow

Fighting a ground fire.

forest fires in epidemic proportions. Surface fires kill young trees and destroy forest litter, which in turn reduces soil fertility.

A burned-over forest.

The best way to fight forest fires is to prevent them. You can help do this by following the rules shown on this page. Once a fire starts, you can help control it by reporting it promptly to the authorities. Many states rely on prompt fire observing and reporting instead of closing down their forests during hazardous seasons and depriving the people of their use. "No smoking, no burning" rules are put into effect for people who use the woods.

Fire Prevention Rules

1. *Matches.* Be sure matches are out. Break them in two before throwing them away. (If the match isn't out, you'll find out when you break it!)
2. *Tobacco.* Be sure all pipe ashes and cigar or cigarette stubs are *dead out* before throwing them away. Never throw them out of a car or into brush, leaves, or needles.
3. *Campfire.* Before building a campfire, scrape away all flammable material from a spot 10 feet in diameter. Dig a hole in the center for the fire. Keep the fire small and never build it against trees, logs, or near brush.
4. *Breaking Camp.* Never break camp until the camp fire is out — *dead out* — cold. To put out a campfire, stir the coals while soaking them with water. If the ashes are still warm, the fire is not out. Be sure the last spark is out.
5. *Brush Burning.* Tell the ranger or fire warden when burning brush, trash, and debris. Have plenty of help and fire-fighting tools handy. Never burn trash or grass or brush in windy weather or when there is the slightest danger that the fire will get out of control.

Commercial Forests

U.S. Forest Service

Clear cutting Douglas Fir helps a new crop to reseed itself in the open areas.

Two-thirds of America's forest area is in commercial forest land — that is, land suitable and available for growing continuous crops of sawlogs, pulpwood, or other kinds of timber. The forest industries, which produce lumber for pulp, paper, plywood, or furniture, own about 13 per cent of the commercial forests; the public owns about 27 per cent; and the remaining 60 per cent are owned privately, mostly by small landowners.

It is in the small, privately-owned forests that conservation is most needed. Most small forests are on farms whose owners pay little attention to proper management. Often the farmer accepts an offer for permission to cut all the standing timber on the land with the result that trees are cut indiscriminately.

There are some exceptions, of course. An increasing number of small landowners work in cooperation with state and federal forestry agents. They have learned that they can make wise use of their woodlots and still earn a regular income. As more landowners practice forest conservation, timber resources will be replenished for future generations.

In the past, when forests seemed inexhaustible, the forest industries and almost everyone else cut timber without regard for the future. Some magnificent stands of forest were ruined, perhaps forever. Today, most forest industries have good management on their lands. They use scientific cutting, practice fire control methods, thin out old stands to let in precious sunlight and, where necessary, plant new trees as old ones are removed.

The need for timber grows rapidly each year. Since 1943, forest acreage has increased by more than 32 million acres; yet this is not enough. First, much of the recovered acreage is worn-out farmland which produces poor timber. This land must be restocked with trees before it can produce good quality timber. Second, despite improved conservation practices, 25 per cent of all our timber is still destroyed by fire, disease, or insects. In spite of intensive research to improve the methods of making wood products, only 75 per cent of the tree is used.

Sawlogs and pulp account for about three-quarters of our forest products. Sawlogs are used for building and for furniture; pulp is used mostly for producing paper and paper products. Pulp forests take less time to grow and the quality of wood need not be so high.

If we hope to have enough wood for the future to meet the tremendous growth in demand, we must properly manage our forests to cut our timber losses and improve our methods of production to reduce waste. It can be done if owners, industry, government, and the general public cooperate.

Measuring pines to be cut for pulpwood.
Hardwood trees.

Douglas Fir.

Forest Management

Learning about tree farming in a summer camp.

If all of our forests were managed under good forestry practices (and most of them are not), they could supply our wood products, watershed protection, and recreation facilities for as far ahead as we can see — so long as population increase does not get out of control. How can this be accomplished?

Conservation and an expanded program of forest research are the key to better forestry and forest management. One of the goals of forest research is to find new ways to use all parts of the tree; another is to combat fire, insects, and disease; and a third is to develop better strains of trees from seed. Foresters look for many things in superior trees — fast growth, resistance to disease, tall straight trunks with few knots, and a wood of high density. These characteristics can be controlled in selective planting of forest trees much as they can in developing better flowers, fruits, or vegetables. Scientists are now seeking ways to do this in naturally-grown forest trees.

More than 100 million acres of commercial forest land must be planted or seeded to new trees if commercial timber crops are to be available again within a reasonable time. We now plant only 1¼ million acres annually, of which many trees are lost each year by fire, poor forest management, or natural catastrophes.

Since 1941, the forest industries have promoted the Tree Farm System in which private landowners are encouraged to manage their forests, large or small. Under this program, a company will give free forest management advice to neighboring landowners in return for the first option on the purchase of the timber when it is ready for harvesting. The Tree Farm Program also recognizes that forests are important for recreation and for water, soil, and wildlife conservation.

A tree nursery.

Idaho State Forestry Dept.

The woodlot provides the farmer with wood and a small income.

One of the important ideas in forest management is multiple use of forest land. Under this system, forest areas serve a number of uses, each one fitting in with the other, and none harmful to the land or other resources. Timber production may be the major value of a forest, but its recreation, watershed protection, livestock grazing, wildlife habitat, and even limited mining possibilities also can be developed. Another forest may have recreation or watershed protection as its primary value and wood production as a secondary use.

Pruning to yield clear lumber.

U.S. Forest Service

The need for keeping our forests open and fit for recreation should not be underestimated. Solitude is one of our greatest needs and no place provides solitude like a forest. There you can get away from the crowds, pavement, cars, phones, and television. The harsh noises of city living give way to the sounds of birds, insects, rustling leaves, and rippling brooks; to the splash of a canoe in a glistening lake or the complete silence of an offshore fisherman. Even a forest picnic area offers a welcome change as a cool, refreshing haven from the crowded city. We can cook outdoors and lie down and watch the clouds drift by through a canopy of leaves or pine needles.

Forests are an important natural resource. They provide wood, watershed and soil protection, wildlife habitat, recreation, a place for grazing animals. With the cooperation of private landowners, industry, and the public, all of these benefits can be secured for this and future generations through good management and planning.

From Logs To Lumber

Logging — the cutting and hauling of trees to mills — was one of the earliest commercial activities on the North American continent. The first settlers had to log the hard way; that is, they cut the trees by hand and hauled them by oxen. The ax was the only tool for felling trees until about 1875, when the crosscut saw came into use. Just before that, a blacksmith in Maine invented the peavey, a logging tool that greatly improved man's ability to roll logs. Winter was the best "logging time," because logs were skidded to water, farm or mill; and skidding was easiest on snow or ice. Gasoline and electric chain saws have replaced the crosscut saw and reduced the amount of ax work on limbs, which can be more quickly cut from a downed tree with a chain saw. The ox and horse have become almost obsolete since power-driven tractors and logging cables now drag the logs with greater efficiency. (They also do more damage to the land and the remaining trees.)

In a well-managed forest, foresters estimate the amount of timber that can be cut while still keeping the forest productive. This is called "cruising" because a "cruiser" first looks over the area and measures the diameter, height, and kind of trees on several sample plots. From these samples, he figures the total amount of timber the forest will yield. Then a logging plan is prepared to show where roads and skid trails can be located with least damage to soil. Roads are essential in the forest. Many are built wide for use by the large trucks needed to haul logs.

Marking mature trees.

Weyerhaeuser Co.

Trimming the crown.

Weyerhaeuser Co.

Loading logs for the trip to the mill.

Weyerhaeuser Co.

The trees marked for harvest are felled, trimmed, and "bucked" into log lengths for easy handling. In the East this length is usually 8 to 16 feet; in the West it is 12 to 40 feet. Western logging operations require heavier equipment.

The logs are skidded by tractor or cables to "landings," where they are loaded on trucks and taken directly to the mills or to large bodies of water where they are assembled into rafts and towed to the mills.

At the mills, the logs are sprayed or washed in mill ponds, then put through revolving bark-removing machines. The stripped, clean logs then are sawed into lumber or, in a paper mill, slivered into chips by powerful rotating blades. In large mills, the logs are cut into lumber by the head-saw or bandsaw, a wide strip of steel with saw teeth. The logs, tightly clamped onto a movable saw carriage, travel back and forth against the saw and are cut into boards of various thicknesses and widths. In small mills, the saw carriage travels against a large circular saw running at high speed.

In large mills, a second operation reduces the larger lumber boards to smaller sizes after they have been squared-up by the headsaw. There are also edgers for squaring edges and reducing boards to a standard width. The boards are then sorted by grade or quality. Better grades of board are usually kiln-dried under heat and then planed and packaged for shipping. Small mills usually sell their lumber "green," and others "air-dry" it in outdoor piles before sale.

Weyerhaeuser Co.

Logs are de-barked and shipped.

Weyerhaeuser Co.

From logs to lumber.

Paper From Wood

International Paper Co.

Producing pulp.

International Paper Co.

 Wet end of the Fourdrinier machine.

Paper is one of our most valuable commodities made from trees. The word comes from the Latin, *papyrus,* which describes a plant fiber that the Egyptians pressed together as writing material. Papyrus, however, was not an early form of paper; for true paper is made by pulverizing fibers, mixing them with water, draining off the water with a sieve-like screen, and spreading the matted fiber to dry as a sheet on the screen.

This process, using wood fibers, was invented by a Chinese named Ts'ai Lun about 105 A. D. Then in 751, the Moslems captured a Chinese paper mill in Samarkand, and 400 years later the Europeans finally learned to make paper at a mill in Xativa, Spain. The first American paper mill was built near Philadelphia in 1690.

All the stages in papermaking were performed by hand until the 19th century, when the Fourdrinier paper machine was invented. A modern version of this machine — often a city block long and several stories high is still used to make paper.

Paper starts as a log. Each ounce of each log contains about 13 million cellulose fibers which must be separated and then, with the help of water, intertwined in a single sheet to form paper. First the logs are fed into the "chipper" where rotating steel blades reduce them to chips the size of breakfast cereal. This takes less than three seconds. The chips are sent to ten-story-high "digesters" where chemicals and steam remove resins and lignin, a substance in the wood that binds the cellulose fibers.

The separated fibers — now called pulp — are cleaned and bleached. Then the "furnish" (any necessary dyes or additives) is added. The pulp is now 99 per cent water and 1 per cent fiber and furnish. This mixture is sprayed onto the moving screens of the Fourdrinier machine, where the water drains away and is squeezed out, leaving a thin sheet of matted fibers — paper. At the end of the machine the paper is dried, coated, and trimmed.

The paper industry is one of the largest in the country. Besides producing the paper for books, magazines, newspapers, and letters, it makes paper and cardboard for boxes, containers, packages, cartons, bags, tissues, wrappers, tickets, catalogs, wallboards, stamps, even dollar bills. The industry uses about 45 million tons of pulp a year to fill the demand for paper. A single Sunday issue of a large newspaper may require all the pulpwood from 75 acres of land!

The United States Forest Service estimates that by the year 2000 we will need three times as much pulpwood as we do now. Since 90 per cent of that wood must come from America's forests, we can hope to meet the need only if good management is practiced.

International Paper Co.

Dry end of the paper machine.

International Paper Co.

Finished paper.

U.S. Forest Service

U.S. Forest Service

Logging and fishing in a National Forest.

National Forests

The National Forests were established in 1897 under an Act of Congress which outlined a system of organization and management of selected forest reserves by an agency of the Department of Agriculture. Provided that good conservation practices are followed, the timber on this land can be sold and cut and the grazing land can be leased for livestock range. The guiding philosophy of the Forest Service is that all land is to be devoted to its most productive use for the permanent good of the whole people, and not for temporary benefit of individuals or companies. Where conflicting interests must be reconciled, the question will always be decided from the standpoint of "the greatest good to the

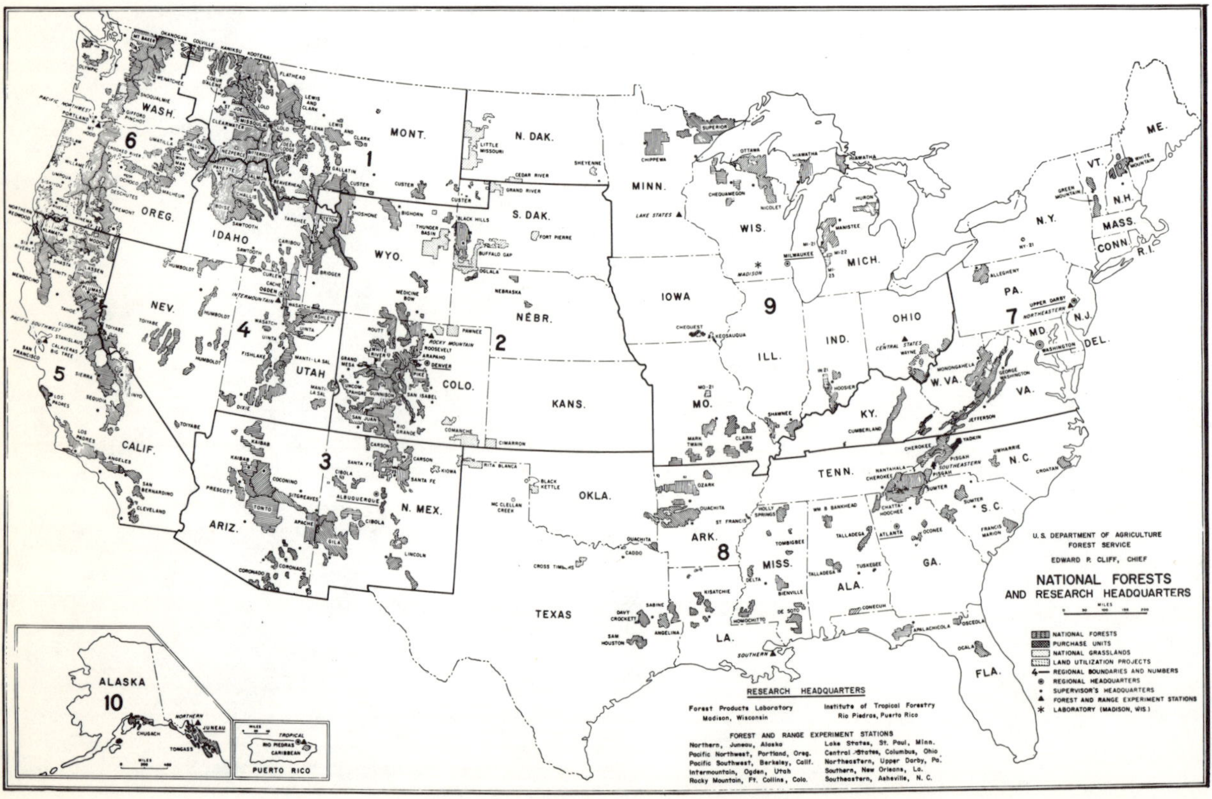

A map showing National Forests and National Grasslands.

Microwave relay station in a National Forest.

Gas compressor pumping station leased to a natural gas company.

greatest number in the long run."

Today there are 154 National Forests, 182 million acres of land owned and operated by the American people. The forests contain one-third of the nation's sawtimber and one-sixth of its commercial forest land. Eighty per cent of the National Forests are in the West. In fact, most of the water in the western states comes from National Forest watersheds — which also provide outdoor recreation areas in that part of the nation.

The National Forests are under the direct supervision of forest rangers. The first rangers were cowboys, trappers, and woodsmen — outdoorsmen who knew and loved the forests and ranges. They had little education but knew how to deal with ranchers, miners, hunters, loggers, and other people who used — and abused — the lands at the time.

Today's rangers have been educated at forestry schools. They have a foundation in botany, chemistry, zoology, ecology, industrial arts, and economics. They are trained to manage the timber, range, water, recrea-

tion, and wildlife resources of the forests "for the permanent good of the whole people."

The government itself does no commercial logging. National forest timber is sold at auction to the highest bidder, companies or individuals who then remove the timber under the rangers' supervision. Mining and grazing rights are also leased.

Each year, the National Forests bring in more than a hundred million dollars in fees; twenty-five per cent of the money is returned to the state in which the forests are located. These fees are income and do not include the value of the water and recreation resources. If they did, the figure would be more like $250 million. But no amount of money can compensate for the protection these forests give to our watersheds. Without this protection, the United States could not continue as a world power of the first rank.

Forest areas are also owned and maintained by state and county governments. They are often open to the public for camping, fishing, swimming, and hunting.

The National Parks

Vermilion Lake,
Banff, Canada.

Each year, more than 100 million people from large cities, small cities, towns, and farms enjoy the natural beauty of 200 areas of the National Park System in 50 states, in Puerto Rico, and the Virgin Islands. Within the National Parks (of which there are 32), there are natural features — lakes, forests, glaciers, geysers, or canyons — historical areas, and recreational areas.

The National Park System is a series of great outdoor museums where visitors may admire natural beauty, learn about the parks through self-guided trails or ranger talks, and relax by fishing, swimming, and camping. When the National Park Service of the United States Department of the Interior was established in 1916, its purpose was to conserve the "scenery and the natural and historic objects and the wildlife, as well as provide for the enjoyment of the same in such manner and by such means as will leave them unimpaired for the enjoyment of future generations."

Every man, woman, and child in the nation should have an opportunity to visit the national parks. They occupy 26 million acres, which comprise only three-fourths of one per cent of the total land area of the nation. Each park has its distinctive beauty and each tells a story of ages long past. Crater Lake, Oregon was formed from an active volcano; Isle Royal, Michigan is a forested island in the midst of Lake Superior; Sequoia in California is the site of the oldest and largest living trees in the world; Bryce, Utah has sculptured rock formations in vivid shades of pink; Grand Canyon tells a story of erosion over billions of years caused by the meandering Colorado River and the rise and fall of ancient seas.

A naturalist has called the parks, "a breathing place for the nation's lungs." The policy of the National Park Service is to preserve nature as created, in a setting which large numbers of visitors can enjoy. Areas within the parks are protected against commercial use for logging, grazing, or power production by the 1920 Federal Power Commission Act.

Some groups are trying to put national park sites to use for hydroelectric plants. At each session, Congress is faced with proposals to flood

Old Faithful Geyser, Yellowstone
National Park.

Grand Canyon National Park.

canyons, create man-made lakes, and build electric power plants. It is argued that such projects would increase the available electricity, bring in revenue, and add boating and fishing facilities for the general public. Conservationists, however, oppose such encroachment on public land as a violation of the public trust. Even within the Department of the Interior, which administers the park system, there are opposing points of view.

Take the Upper Colorado River Basin Project as an example. Upon the recommendation of the Bureau of Reclamation and against the appeals of the National Park Service (both in the Department of the Interior), Glen Canyon and Flaming Gorge Dams in the Grand Canyon National Monument were built.

Each dam provides for water storage from the Colorado River to be used to generate electricity. Glen Canyon, shown here, is over 700 feet high. Lake Powell, which was created from the backed-up river, can store 27,000,000 acre-feet of water. Critics claim that the lake has not been able to store this amount of water and, besides, it has caused a tremendous amount of water loss by evaporation.

Marble Canyon Dam, Reservoir, and Power Plant are under consideration as part of the Lower Colorado River Basin Project. If you could cast a vote for or against the construction of dams in national parks, how would you arrive at a decision? It is very important that all taxpayers keep informed about such matters even though they may be located far away.

Glen Canyon Dam.

Point Reyes National Seashore.

Wilderness Areas

U.S. Forest Service

Bob Marshall Wilderness Area, Montana.

In our eagerness to make the best use of soil, water, forests, wildlife, and minerals for material benefit, it has become obvious that part of our natural heritage must be preserved as wildlands. Scattered throughout all regions of the United States are sections of unspoiled wilderness preserved for future generations as monuments to America's varied landscapes.

Wilderness areas are just what the name implies. A wilderness area established by law is accessible to the public only by foot, horseback, or canoe or rowboat. Motorized travel into it is not permitted. No timber may be cut, but some fishing, hunting, and camping are allowed. There are no roads, except for trails, no buildings or other recreational facilities. A wilderness area is intended as a preserve to be retained much as nature made it, to be used as a place of quiet and solitude, a source of pleasure and inspiration. It is also a laboratory in which naturalists, geologists, conservationists, and many other people may study the interrelationships between plants, animals, weather, land, and water. Wilderness areas are an important part of every culture and their preservation is planned by all nations.

Most of the wilderness areas are within the National Forests, where more than nine million acres in 54 different tracts have been given permanent protection under the Wilderness Act of 1964. About six million additional acres of National Forest land are being considered for inclusion under the Act. Some small areas of the National Parks and large areas in the public domain in Alaska are also being studied.

Some areas, which have somehow retained their natural characteristics in spite of civilization's advance, are preserved by state and federal agencies. State lands are not included in the national wilderness system, although some of them, such as the Forest Preserve of New York State, are as much wilderness as some of the designated federal areas. Conservation organizations sometimes acquire wildlands to protect them. Dome Island in Lake George, New York was acquired by the Nature Conservancy to save it from commercial development. The Sierra Club wages a continuous struggle to preserve the giant redwood trees of California and the wilderness areas of Grand Canyon from encroachment by industry. The first wilderness waterway, the Allagash River, was established in 1966 by the State of Maine. Among the natural formations in need of protection are seashores. At the time of the dedication of Cape Cod National Seashore in 1966, the Secretary of the Interior remarked:

"We who have chopped and mined and built and machined our way to wealth and power now grope out from our cities . . . . for something we cannot forget. Beyond the noise and the asphalt and ugly architecture, we yearn for the long waves and beach grass; we see white wings on morning air, and in the afternoon, the shadows cast by the doorways of history." (Secretary Stewart L. Udall)

John Muir Wilderness Area, California.

U.S. Forest Service

A protected herd of buffalo.

CHAPTER 6

WILDLIFE

Like all our natural resources, wildlife on the North American continent was so abundant at the time of settlement that Americans thought it would last forever. So they killed animals indiscriminately, first for food and hides, then for "sport." Because they knew nothing of wildlife needs, they destroyed the habitat upon which wildlife depends.

Some species of animals, like the passenger pigeon, were destroyed entirely. The passenger pigeon was once so numerous that when formations flew over an area, they often darkened the skies. This animal is now extinct, killed by thoughtless hunters. It is doubtful, however, that it could have survived in modern America because of changes in its habitat. Other animals, such as the buffalo, were hunted nearly to extinction. The buffalo was the chief source of support for the Indians of the Great Plains. They ate the meat and used the hides for clothing and shelter. They carved the horns into spoons and ornaments, used the dried tendons as bowstrings, boiled the hooves into glue, and even burned the dried dung as fuel. At one time, 60 million of these animals roamed the country from Pennsylvania to the Pacific Coast.

As westward expansion pushed the bison herds further and further west, buffalo hunting became both a business and a fashionable sport. Whole herds were slaughtered. In 1874, indignant Congressmen passed a bill to stop the slaughter. The bill never became a law because President Grant, a good general but a weak president, did not sign the bill, and the matter was soon forgotten. By 1907, only about 200 bison (buffalo) remained of the original 60 million. Some of these were rounded up and preserved by conservation groups, l i k e the American Bison Society. Forty animals were sent to the Bronx Zoo in New York City. Later, 15 of these — seven bulls and eight cows — were sent back to the West to federal wildlife preserves to start new herds. There are now about 12,000 buffalo living under protection in these areas and in Alaska.

Of course, the growth of cities has affected our wildlife resources. The more cities, suburbs, railroads, steel mills and highways, the less room and food for wildlife. That is one reason why it is so important to set aside open areas where wildlife can flourish and man can enjoy its presence in the natural habitat. In the name of "progress," marshes have been eliminated to create land for building, streams have been criss-crossed and forests sliced up by superhigh-

ways to speed up travel. Such progress costs much more than most people realize.

When we dry up marshes, we upset the ecology of a region. Marsh animals either go elsewhere or die, and their absence affects the balance of plants and soil. When we change the course of streams or discharge industrial wastes in them, we destroy or evict the fish populations. You can list for yourself the kinds of animals that are dispossessed when forests are cut down. Wildlife and open areas are national treasures that should be conserved for posterity. Like all resources — natural as well as human — the conservation of one depends upon the conservation of others.

Raccoon.

The Predator Myth

Bobcat.

U.S. Forest Service

For many years, we slaughtered our wildlife wantonly without thinking of the consequences. Then, when we realized that we were dangerously depleting a valuable n a t u r a l resource, we took steps to protect our animals. But the steps were in the wrong direction. To protect animals such as deer and beaver, we began killing wolves, coyotes, bobcats, and eagles that prey on weaker wildlife. These predators have a definite place in the balance of nature and, except in unusual cases, should not be promiscuously killed as a wildlife protection measure.

Nature has a way of reproducing the species, whether it be mammals or plants. Her formula is to produce enough young so that annual losses from disease, old age, or enemies will maintain a healthy and vigorous supply and keep the species alive. A classic example of the perils of tampering with the ecology of a region occurred in what is now the Kaibab National Forest near the Grand Canyon in Arizona. In 1906, public deer hunting was prohibited and war was declared on mountain lions, wolves, coyotes, and other predatory animals that fed on deer. The deer population of the area at the time was about 4,000. By 1924, the number had increased to 100,000 — too many for the available food supply — and, in the winter of 1924, thousands of animals starved to death. Hunting was reinstated and, for a few years, about 1,000 deer were killed off annually. In 1930, the population had dropped to about 20,000 deer; by 1940, it was 10,000, a little more than twice what it had been in 1906. Actually, only a few thousand had been killed by hunters and predators; starvation had claimed the rest.

Competent biologists have urged for a long time that habitat improvement rather than predator control is the greatest need in wildlife management. But their appeals fell on deaf ears — until after World War II. Many people now recognize that habitat improvement is important, but in many areas the myth persists through books, newspaper reports, and magazine articles that predators cause a scarcity of wildlife.

Some of the prejudice against predators comes from ranchers whose cattle and sheep have been preyed upon by individual mountain lions and grizzly bears. Instead of seeking out the guilty animals, these ranchers exert influence and cause state laws to be passed to have all of these animals killed. One example: the fate of the grizzly bear is in doubt. Of course, he preys upon cattle and sheep; but he would just as soon kill a deer, elk, or buffalo for food. He simply finds grazing domestic animals easier prey.

Predators perform a useful service in the wild community. They pick off injured, diseased, or aged animals whose removal is necessary for the survival of the healthier animals. When disease is rampant, or animals are hampered in their movements by heavy snows and ice, predators help to reduce and keep their number in balance with the food supply. They also kill off large numbers of rodents which would otherwise compete with the grazing animals for grass. Temporary control of predators may be justified in some places and under certain circumstances; but the wanton killing of these animals threatens their survival.

Wildlife Habitat -- Key To Abundance

The idea of conserving wildlife through improving its habitat is a recent one. Americans became concerned about the wanton destruction of wildlife around 1900. Among the first conservation remedies was the prevention of hunting and killing of predators, as we have seen. The next steps were to set aside game refuges and restock streams and forests. Many experts considered this the best solution to wildlife conservation, and some misguided people still agree.

It does not help much to stock fish in streams where the natural habitat has been destroyed by pollution, the silting over of spawning beds, or the lack of natural fish food. When pheasants and quail, for example are introduced into areas where the food, climate or shelter are unsatisfactory, they soon disappear. Waterfowl are killed not only by hunters' guns, but because their nesting grounds have been destroyed by big dams, fire, overgrazing, drainage, land filling, or water pollution.

Wis. Conservation Dept.

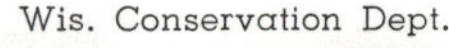

We have also learned that the combination of food, shelter, and water determines not only the number of birds, fish, or other animals that can live there, but also their quality. When the food supply is low, wildlife quality declines and starvation results.

No land has unlimited capacity for the production of food and shelter for animals. Generally, however, habitat can be improved through carefully coordinated soil, water, forest, and wildlife management practices. As habitat improves, wildlife numbers increase. They may then exceed the ability of the area to support them. It is then that hunting can help to restore the balance between habitat and animals.

Two conditions are necessary for good wildlife conservation — good habitat and a balanced harvest through hunting. These must, of course, be accompanied by well-designed game laws, including carefully regulated open seasons. Re-

stocking may sometimes be necessary to start the buildup of a wildlife crop. But it is expensive and ineffective in the long run. With a little help from man, nature can do a better and more economical job of saving our wildlife.

Forests And Wildlife

U.S. Bureau of Biological Survey

When beavers flood an area with their dams a few animals are trapped and shipped to a new location.

Brown Brothers

Wild areas and wildlife are closely related, and one of the best places to observe the relationship is in the forests.

Hardwood forests predominate in the eastern United States. Under reasonably good management, they provide (in addition to timber products) food for wildlife — mast (nuts) from oaks, hickories, chestnuts, walnuts, and beech; and fruits and berries from the gum, grape, dogwood, persimmon, and other vines and shrubs. Hardwood trees also make good dens for squirrels and raccoons, and some of the larger trees are homes for the black bear.

Evergreen or coniferous forests, which are interspersed with the hardwood forests, furnish poorer wildlife habitat and a less varied food supply. The wild animals there usually differ from those in the hardwood stands. For example, more deer and turkey are found in hardwood forests than in dense evergreen stands, while the snowshoe hare and the spruce grouse prefer evergreens.

In mixed forests, there is generally a greater variety of wildlife, but not always greater numbers than in hardwood forests.

In the West, the forests are largely coniferous or evergreen, but many are "open" and interspersed with meadows, brush, and open grasslands. Around the edges of these areas are small shrubs, trees, brush, and vines upon which a variety of wildlife live. The food supply in these forests usually favors the larger browsing and grazing animals, such as deer and elk.

Originally, all American forests supported some kind of wildlife such as bear, deer, squirrels, beaver, cougars, and wolves — though not in the numbers some historians have claimed. Indian tribes and the early settlers found different types of grouse in all areas except in the coastal plain in the South and Southeast. Elk ranged everywhere except in the South. Beaver and turkeys were found from New England to Colorado and Arizona.

Wanton slaughter caused a change in the pattern. Elk, for example, disappeared from the East and from many parts of the West about 1870. Trapping had practically eliminated the beaver throughout the nation, although he has come back strong in some areas.

Professional hunters and local bounty systems eliminated the gray timber wolf in the lake states, except for one small area. Mountain lions and cougars are now only found in some of the rougher and wilder sections of the West. The last grizzly bear in California was killed in 1922, and that species is now confined to Alaska, Montana, Wyoming, Idaho, and parts of Canada.

The clearing of forests for agriculture or logging followed by burning has a mixed effect on wildlife habitat. Such activity usually results in more borders or edges around the forest, and the shrubs and bushes that grow there provide food and shelter for deer and grouse. Other animals, however, are deprived of the food supply found in older trees. Tree squirrels find less food and fewer dens; and other species, such as the martin and fisher, cannot survive at all in the new environment.

Logging, burning, or grazing in a forest affects the entire ecology of a region. Unless carefully controlled, these activities may raise water temperature and increase flooding which covers fish spawning beds with silt and thus reduces insect populations upon which fish feed. Since trout require cold water, trout streams in the forest are ruined for fishing. What man does affects nature, and the result affects him.

The Silent Killers

Since World War II, hundreds of new chemicals have been developed to help control insects, plant diseases, and obnoxious plants in order to reduce losses to agriculture. The chemicals generally have done the job — but at a cost which we are now beginning to realize. These chemicals pose a serious hazard to all forms of wildlife, to say nothing of their effects upon human life.

Pesticides and insecticides are used in staggering amounts. More than one billion pounds, worth one billion dollars, are produced yearly for application to American land, about triple the amount produced in 1958. So, the danger to fish, animals, and

man has increased accordingly, and continues to increase at a rapid pace. Airplanes are used to spread larger amounts of the insecticides over wider areas.

Pesticides cause both direct and indirect damage to wildlife. Fish and other vertebrates that live in water are particularly sensitive to chemicals and can tolerate only very small amounts of them. Birds can survive with larger amounts, and mammals can withstand even heavier doses. Insecticides used to control forest insects will kill or maim birds and mammals unless very carefully and sparingly applied. Many birds — the American eagle among them — show

Standard Oil Co. (N.J.)

The record of pesticides prompts the question of whether their use in such large quantities is justified, except as a last resort and under very strict controls. Although the directions often state that they should be used "within safe limits," most scientists admit that there is no agreement on what the safe limits may be. All pesticides are harmful to a degree.

An important method of controlling pests is through biological control. It is relatively inexpensive, it is permanent, and it leaves no harmful chemical residues. Birds feed on insects. So do spiders and some mammals, and some insects feed on others. In biological control, the idea is to bring the proper predator to the offending insect. For example, the shrew feeds on the cocoons of the sawfly and has been successfully used in Canada to help control this tree pest. What is needed is more research, not more chemical killers.

less and less capacity to produce young. Tests have shown that chemicals reduce the fertility of birds and many scientists believe that this is the result of feeding on spray-contaminated worms, seeds, and berries.

Insecticides used to spray shade trees are stronger than those used in forests. Spraying in Michigan and Wisconsin in 1959 for the control of the Dutch elm tree disease killed up to 90 per cent of the song birds in the sprayed communities and failed to save the elm trees!

During the 1950's, chemicals were used to control the fire ant in sections of the South. Studies of treated areas after application of the insecticides revealed dead raccoons, rabbits, opposums, song birds, quail, turkeys — all with evidence of the chemicals in their bodies. Domestic turkeys in the treated area produced no young; yet reproduction was normal in untreated areas, showing an indirect effect on these birds. But the fire ant lived on.

Wis. Conservation Dept.

Death In The Water

Fed. Water Pollution Control Admin.

Like our birds and small animals, fish have been killed by the millions by careless and often unnecessary chemical spraying.

Even a tiny amount of insecticide in a stream will kill fish. In Canada, forest spraying with a half-pound of DDT per acre to control the spruce budworm killed almost all of the young salmon in portions of the Mir-amicki River, New Brunswick. Two years later, the area was again sprayed, with the same results. In Montana, aerial application of DDT for control of the same insect pest had little effect on trout until two years later, when the population showed a decline of 75 per cent. The fish were affected for 85 miles downstream from the sprayed areas.

U.S. Forest Service

Almost any kind of water pollution is fatal to fish. Near San Diego, California, almost 40 million anchovies died in 1962 because someone dumped a large amount of paint-making chemicals near the harbor entrance. The dead fish weighed about 945 tons and filled an area 10 feet wide, three feet deep and 1,000 feet long. That same year in the Anacostia River near Washington, D. C., three million fish were killed when raw sewage was dumped into the river in large quantities. Highway construction had interrupted the normal system of sewage disposal.

Other pollutants that affect fish are detergents, oil, steam, acids, even milk. Sometimes water pollution is the result of an accident, as when a tank car falls into a stream or chemicals leak from faulty equipment into drainage channels. But more often, water pollution is caused by indifference or neglect.

Short-sightedness t a k e s many forms. In Tierra Verde, a group of Florida islands, real estate developers are creating land by dredging from the surroundings some of the finest marine nursery grounds in the South. Once it is used as land fill, this lush bay bottom and the marine life it supports will be lost forever. Boca Ciego Bay near St. Petersburg was once a similar area; now it is merely a lifeless canal system flanked by waterfront homes.

If we are to conserve our fish and marine life for future generations, our water resources need to be carefully managed.

Managing Wildlife Resources

U.S. Bureau of Biological Survey

Conservation of wildlife is a job that requires federal, state, and private landowners' cooperation. There are, however, areas in which public or private interests assume the primary responsibility.

At the federal level, the Bureau of Sport Fisheries and Wildlife of the Fish and Wildlife Service, Department of the Interior, is responsible for the conservation of fish, birds, mammals and their habitat. The Forest Service of the Department of Agriculture is responsible for the management of wildlife in the National Forests. Each of these agencies works in cooperation with the individual states which control game seasons, determine bag and catch limits, issue game licenses, and perform other functions that are properly the responsibility of the states.

Other federal agencies, such as the Bureau of Reclamation, the Bureau of Land Management, the Soil Conservation Service, and the Army Corps of Engineers, are also involved in wildlife management. The Bureau of Sport Fisheries and Wildlife watches over migratory bird populations through a system of waterfowl refuges and law enforcement programs along the migrating flyways. By international agreement, these routes are protected along areas in northern Canada, Alaska, and South America. Hunting seasons are based on surveys that determine the number of birds that will travel the flyways each year and the number that may be safely taken.

The spread of cities outward into the suburbs often requires that the breeding areas of waterfowl be filled in. The Bureau of Sport Fisheries and Wildlife tries to preserve at least part of such habitats. When a dam is to be built, the Bureau insists that a nearby area be found or even built to take the place of the habitat that is ruined by water impoundment. For some migrating waterfowl, the deep water submerges food and animal supplies and nesting places. Floating islands or poles on which baskets or tubs have been attached are welcome nesting sites for Canada geese.

The Bureau of Sport Fisheries and Wildlife, in cooperation with individual states, has saved one endangered species, the Trumpeter Swan,

U.S. Dept. of Interior

and is trying to save the Aleutian Canada goose, the Everglades kite, and the whooping crane — all of which are having a hard struggle to survive.

The Bureau also operates a hundred fish hatcheries from which millions of fish are stocked each year in waters on federal lands. It helps to develop sport fishing on Indian reservations by designing fisheries and showing Indians where and how to build the lakes. It demonstrates proper stocking and management of the fish stock. The Office of Foreign Activities advises and helps nations with newly-established natural resource programs. Africa, with its great wildlife and fisheries problems and lack of trained biologists and land managers, has been the focal point for most of the activities of this office.

The Bureau of Commercial Fisheries of the Department of the In-terior concerns itself primarily with salt-water fish as food for man. Scientists believe that fish foods are the major hope for feeding the earth's burgeoning populations. A major project of the Bureau is research involving the production of a uniform nutritious fish protein concentrate, known as FPC. This is a tasteless, odorless, dehydrated flour that could add vital protein to the meager diets of the two billion people of the world who are chronically undernourished.

One important conservation activity of the Bureau is the management of the annual whale and fur seal harvests. It also studies the fish resources of the Great Lakes and of rivers in which high dams and storage reservoirs are obstacles to migratory fish, such as the salmon of the Pacific Northwest. The Bureau carries on research dealing with fish disease, the culture of oysters and clams, and the use of fish products in industry.

Conservation By The States

In the long run, the fate of most wildlife in the United States depends upon the respective states rather than upon the federal government. Wildlife, with the exception of waterfowl and other migratory birds, is the property of the state in which it is found. Therefore, except for migratory waterfowl, the states actually establish the policies that govern wildlife conservation in America.

Since there are 50 states, there are as many different ways of doing the job. Some states are doing it well; others are doing it poorly; but in no state is there a program that meets

U.S. Forest Service

U.S. Forest Service

U.S. Soil Conservation Service

the full needs of the natural resource it seeks to conserve. This is not the fault of the sincere men and women employed by the state fish and game departments. The failure is due mainly to pressure groups who prevent the necessary laws from being passed. They are successful because the general public does not understand the need to eliminate politics from state conservation programs. The future, then, lies with the people within the respective states.

The states have, indeed, come a long way from those early days when their only job was to enforce game laws and operate game farms. Several state wildlife agencies are directed by trained biologists who attempt to develop conservation programs based on sound practice and knowledge. Some states have research programs. Some states are acquiring wetlands and other wildlife areas. In some, there are landowner cooperative conservation programs. Most states have a program of public education on the need for wildlife conservation. They have even changed the name of game wardens to "conservation officers." Most important, the trend is to work for habitat improvement on both public and private lands.

Private land containing fields, ranges, and woods make up 60 per cent of the United States. The way in which owners manage their properties determines the fate of much of our wildlife. As always, the care of habitat is the key, and the landowner can either damage or improve habitat by his use of it.

Most conservation practices which are good for farming and ranching are also good for wildlife. There are exceptions, however. For example, some farm and ranch owners tend to increase their usable land by draining swamps and marshes. This destroys the breeding and nesting grounds of many birds, fish, and waterfowl. In states where little privately-owned waterfowl habitat remains, as New York, the danger is more from the filling in of such lands for industrial and residential use than from drainage.

Some farm and ranch owners provide new homes for waterfowl that have been displaced. In South Dakota, 100,000 acres of small man-made ponds attract almost 150,000 ducks yearly. Many of these ponds are stocked with fish and provide fishing for the owners and other sportsmen.

Often fields are joined to forests on a farm by a strip of unproductive land. Such strips, when planted to suitable shrubs, provide food as well as shelter for small birds and mammals. In the Midwest, farmers may delay mowing the sloping ends of contoured and strip-cropped fields so that the nests of the ring-necked pheasant will not be disturbed. These birds are a valuable farm crop. In the Great Plains, windbreaks of trees and shrubs are particularly favored as nesting places for the mourning dove and provide habitat for wildlife, especially rabbits. On western ranches, deer, elk, and antelope graze on the same open range as do livestock. These lands can be managed to take care of both livestock and wildlife. Since livestock is the cash crop, stockmen give first consideration to cattle or sheep.

Where there is watershed protection and flood control, the fish crop is improved by reducing the amount of silt which goes into streams. Silt covers the spawning beds, damages the fish gills, and covers the rocks, plants, and gravel on which insect larvae breed. The insects, in turn, are food for fish.

Rabbits, grouse, quail, ducks, geese, pheasants, doves, raccoons, squirrels, wild turkey, deer, elk, and antelope are game animals. All of them are found on farms and ranches. In fact, with the possible exception of elk, most of the wildlife is grown and hunted on private land used for farming, grazing, or forestry. That is why the owners of farm and ranch land hold the balance for the future of wildlife resource management.

Shrubs provide shelter for deer, rabbits and other wildlife.

Dogwood berries are good food for deer.

U.S. IS FREE WORLD'S BIGGEST MATERIALS CONSUMER...

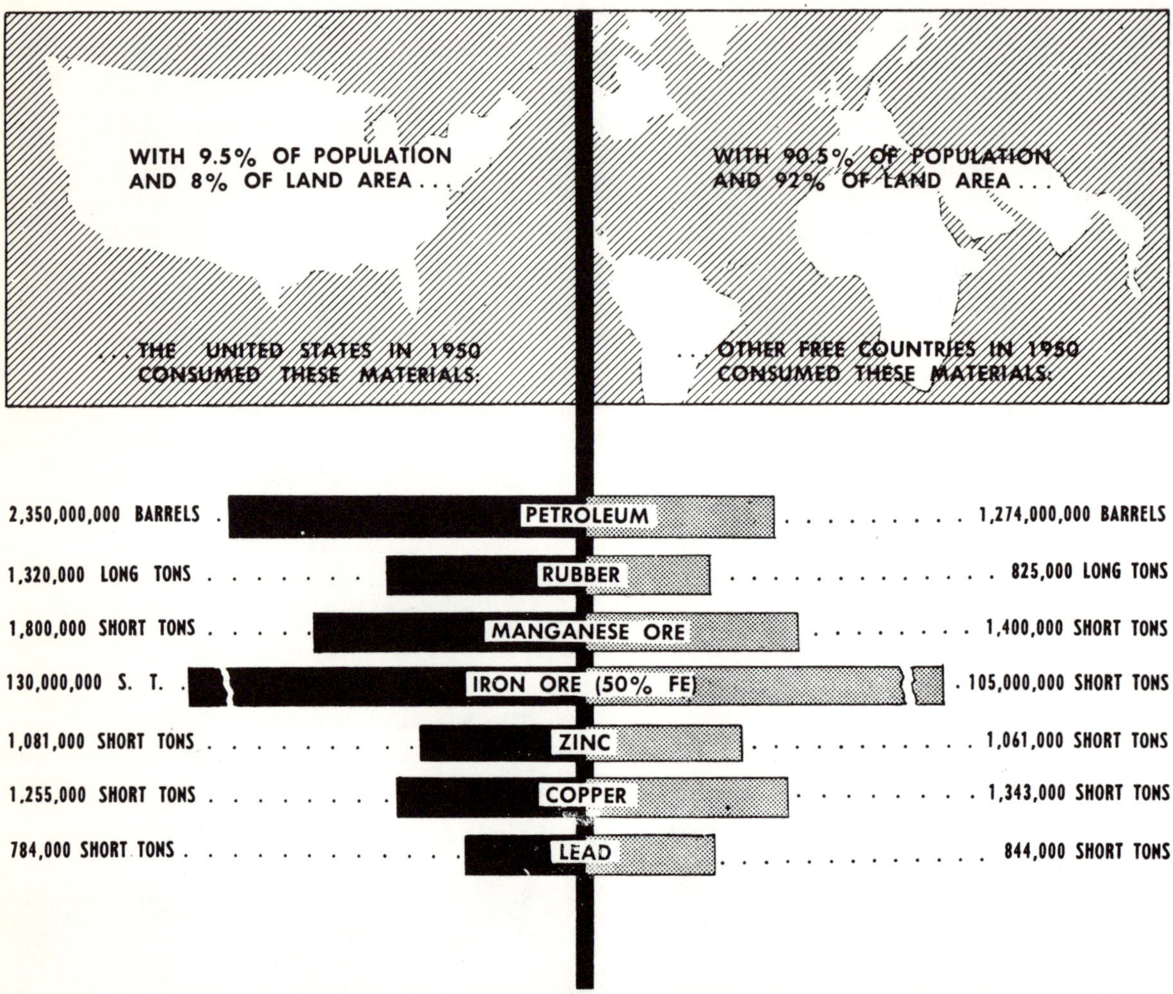

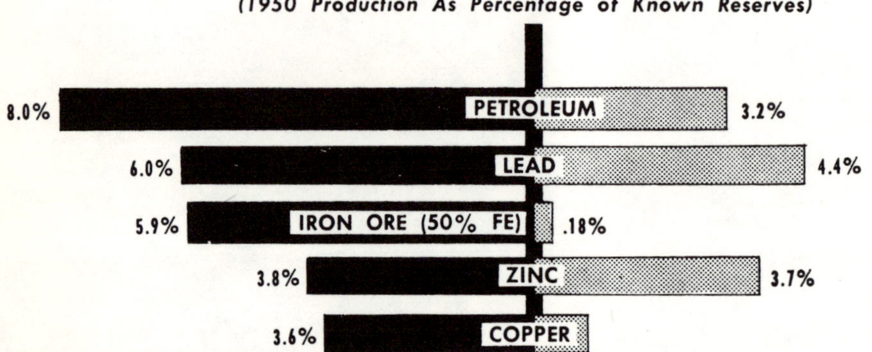

...AND U. S. IS USING UP RESERVES FASTER THAN OTHER COUNTRIES

(1950 Production As Percentage of Known Reserves)

Source: Commodity Studies; PMPC Projection

Joint Council on Economic Education

CHAPTER 7

MINERALS

So far we have discussed the conservation of renewable resources. Under the proper conditions, forests and wildlife reproduce themselves and soil renews its fertility. The amount of water in the water cycle remains constant; and the air we breathe, though it may become polluted, is inexhaustible. Minerals, however, are non-renewable. We cannot plant new minerals as we can new forests; once minerals are taken from the earth, they cannot be replaced.

The minerals we use today were formed millions of years ago. Technically, new minerals constantly are being formed in the earth. But their formation takes millions of years and their total consumption may take only a few thousand, so in practice, minerals are irreplaceable.

There are three broad classes of minerals — metals, non-metals, and fuels (hydrocarbons). The metals usually are found mixed with other chemical elements in ores, among them iron, copper, aluminum, magnesium, nickel, and zinc. Only a few metals, such as gold and silver, are found pure.

Non-metallic minerals, as their name implies, contain no metal or so little as to be insignificant. Metals and non-metals are of inorganic origin, that is, they are formed from rocks or from materials other than plants or animals. Mineral fuels, such as coal, oil and natural gas, are formed from the fats and oil of decayed plants and animals; we therefore describe them as being of organic origin, or fossil fuels.

Metals and fuels are important minerals in an industrial society. But non-metals are important, too. They include sulfur, graphite, gypsum, clay, borax, halite (common salt), talc, asbestos, shale, quartz, diamonds and other gem stones, and hundreds of others. Some of them come ready to use commercially. Talcum powder is ground-up talc; cement is made from ground-up limestone. Gypsum is burned to extract the water and then moistened again as it is used in plaster-board, medical casts and other plaster products. Sand (ground-up quartz) and gravel go directly into construction work after impurities have been washed out.

Many of the minerals perform vital, unseen tasks in our economy. Sulfur and salt, for example, are used in important industrial processes. Diamonds, the hardest substances known, are used in grinding, cutting, and drilling operations.

Mineral conservation practices stress research — to uncover new sources of minerals, to develop more efficient ways of extracting them from their ores, and to devise substitute materials for the minerals in scarce supply. Since minerals are so important to the national economy, laws have been passed to control mineral mining and distribution. Laws at the state and national levels regulate drilling and mining operations of coal, oil, and other minerals. They also specify the materials that must be stockpiled for national defense and for future use.

Coal

Coal is the organic matter of dense, prehistoric tropical forests which has been transformed into its present state by the intense heat and pressure of successive layers of water, silt, and mud over millions of years. There are four kinds of coal — peat, lignite, bituminous, and anthracite. Actually each kind represents a stage in the formation of this valuable mineral.

Peat, the first step in the formation of coal, is fibrous and woody and full of moisture. It is easy to cut and has been used over a long period of time as a low-grade fuel. Right now peat is forming in marshes and bogs in Ireland and in swamps such as the Dismal Swamps of Virginia and North Carolina.

Lignite, the next step in coal formation, is a brown, woody coal with a fairly high moisture content. It is used as a fuel for generating electricity. There are large deposits of lignite in North Dakota. Both peat and lignite are found close to the surface of the earth. If they were deeper, the additional pressure and heat would have transformed them further.

Bituminous (soft) coal is black and blocky. It is the most abundant coal in the world. Soft coal is used to generate more than half of the electric power in the United States. It also is the source of coke, a vital ingredient in steel making.

Anthracite (hard) coal is the final step in coal formation. It is a brilliant black. It is the best quality because it has the fewest impurities and burns longest. It is also the most expensive of the coals because it lies deepest underground, is more difficult to mine, and there is less of it. Can you tell why?

Ancient people knew the value of coal for fuel. Coal was known to the people of biblical times, the Greeks, and early Europeans. Marco Polo reported seeing "black stones" dug from the mountains of China and burned for fuel. Coal played a large part in the rapid development of power-driven machinery in England, making possible the Industrial Revolution. There were abundant supplies of coal for producing steam power and also for the manufacture of the steel needed to build the machines. Coal has remained an important factor in determining a nation's industrial and political power.

The United States today is the world's leading producer of coal. American miners, using cutting and loading machines, produce a greater amount of coal per man than those of other countries in the world. Fewer men are needed today to produce more coal than a generation ago. In 1923, nearly 650,000 miners worked in the bituminous coal mines to pro-

Mining underground.

duce 569 million tons a year. There are about one million persons earning a living from some aspect of the coal industry, although large numbers of miners have been replaced by machines.

Coal is used as fuel in industry, though almost completely replaced by oil as a fuel for homes. It is an important raw material in the manufacture of many chemical products. These include synthetic fibers, plastics, paints, dyes, medicines, detergents, and fertilizers. The bulky nature of coal makes it difficult to transport. Scientists are, therefore, seeking ways of changing coal to liquid and gaseous forms that could be shipped by pipeline. In this form it would compete favorably with the other fuels.

It is estimated that our coal supplies can last 5,000 years. That is a long time in human terms but when you realize that it took millions of years for the coal to form, 5,000 years is not very long.

There are two ways to mine minerals. In one, a shaft or entry is cut through the ground (called the "overburden") to the mineral ore and men or machines tunnel underground to dig out the ore. This is the underground, or shaft, or slope mining. In the other method, large power shovels scoop up the overburden and pile it in mounds, exposing the mineral ore, which is then broken up and carted away. This is called strip mining or surface mining. It is used when the mineral ore lies fairly close to the earth's surface.

Strip mining is safer and less costly than underground mining. It also is far more destructive to water, land, and all that stands on it — the trees,

U.S. Dept. of Interior

Strip mining.

plants, soil, wildlife, even the people that live nearby.

In Illinois, 125,000 acres embracing some of the world's best corn land have been ripped up; in Pennsylvania, 250,000 acres have been left as bleak and barren as a desert; in Virginia, large mountains have been leveled; in West Virginia and Kentucky whole valleys have been torn apart. Wherever strip mining is carried on, there are desolation, broken trees, shattered rock, soil erosion, ugliness, and poverty. The Appalachian hills once were lush with the beauty of forests and rivers and rich in mineral resources; today, the areas stripped of forests as well as minerals, are a land of poverty caused by greed and short-sightedness.

To date almost two million acres of land have been destroyed or severely damaged by strip mining of coal and other minerals. That is poor conservation and, in the long run, bad economics. What is needed is cooperation between state and federal governments to regulate this destructive practice; to make land reclamation compulsory; to prevent strip mining in areas where the terrain is not suited for it, as along steep slopes or where other values — watershed protection, recreation, or natural beauty — are greater than that of mining coal.

A crude form of oil has been known for thousands of years. Noah was supposed to have caulked the ark with oil that had oozed from the ground. Early Egyptians lubricated their chariot wheels with oil; and the Greeks, according to legend, poured it on the sea and set it afire, burning an invading fleet.

In America, the Indians and the early settlers called the crude petroleum that seeped from the ground "rock oil" and used it for almost any illness. It was not until 1850, however, when a successful oil-burning lamp was invented, and oil was used in increasing amounts for industry, that the potential of oil was realized. In 1859 Edwin L. Drake, superintendent of the Pennsylvania Rock Oil Company, started drilling for oil near Titusville, Pennsylvania in the same way that salt wells were drilled. Local people called his efforts "Drake's Folly." Drake persisted and, at about 70 feet, struck oil. He founded a great new industry.

Today, the United States leads the world in oil production, despite the fact that two-thirds of the world's discovered oil reserves are in the Middle East and North Africa. One of the reasons why we lead in oil production is that we began to practice oil conservation about the time of World War I. Leading producing states are Texas, Louisiana, California, and Oklahoma.

Conservation begins with knowledge and we have learned a great deal about oil. No one is certain how oil is formed or how much there is in the world, but its formation is thought to be similar to that of coal. We do know that oil is trapped in reservoirs in the rocks of prehistoric sea beds now overlaid by land.

Early oil producers tapped the reservoirs with as many wells as they could drill to extract as much as possible for themselves. This is poor conservation because oil is stored in the ground without waste, but once it is brought to the surface and stored, there is some waste. Early wells also were allowed to "gush" wastefully.

The underground reservoirs of oil pools are not confined to property lines but may extend across several properties that lie above them.

Modern oil wells are capped immediately to prevent gushing and the oil that is drilled is divided between owners while it is still in the reservoir. In this manner, engineers using modern technology can recover the maximum amount of oil from each pool.

Oil is forced to the surface by the natural pressure from underground gas or water. In the past, when this pressure got too low, the well was abandoned. Today, water or gas may be injected into the pool to get more oil into the wells from the rock. This is called "secondary recovery." In some cases, it increases production two or three times above that which would have been obtained without the extra pressure.

These practices are part of a conservation program that began in 1915, when Oklahoma enacted the first oil and gas conservation law. It stated that waste was "economic waste, underground waste, surface waste and waste over and above the market demand for oil and gas." In 1935, Congress authorized an Interstate Oil Compact which is an oil and gas conservation program. Oil experts estimate that these programs already have produced five billion barrels of oil that would have been otherwise lost and will produce another five billion extra barrels in the future.

Meanwhile, the oil industry has learned to use every drop of crude oil produced. Most of our crude oil is refined into gasoline — which was considered a waste product before the invention of the automobile! Other petroleum products, besides fuel oil and kerosene (the first important product of crude oil), include plastics, synthetic rubber, fertilizers, asphalt, medicines, perfumes, synthetic fibers, and sulfur.

Research continues in the quest for new sources and new uses for petroleum. Scientists hope some day to be able to extract oil economically from shale, a rock so common that in this country alone it would yield trillions of barrels of oil.

Some products of crude oil.

Standard Oil of N.J.

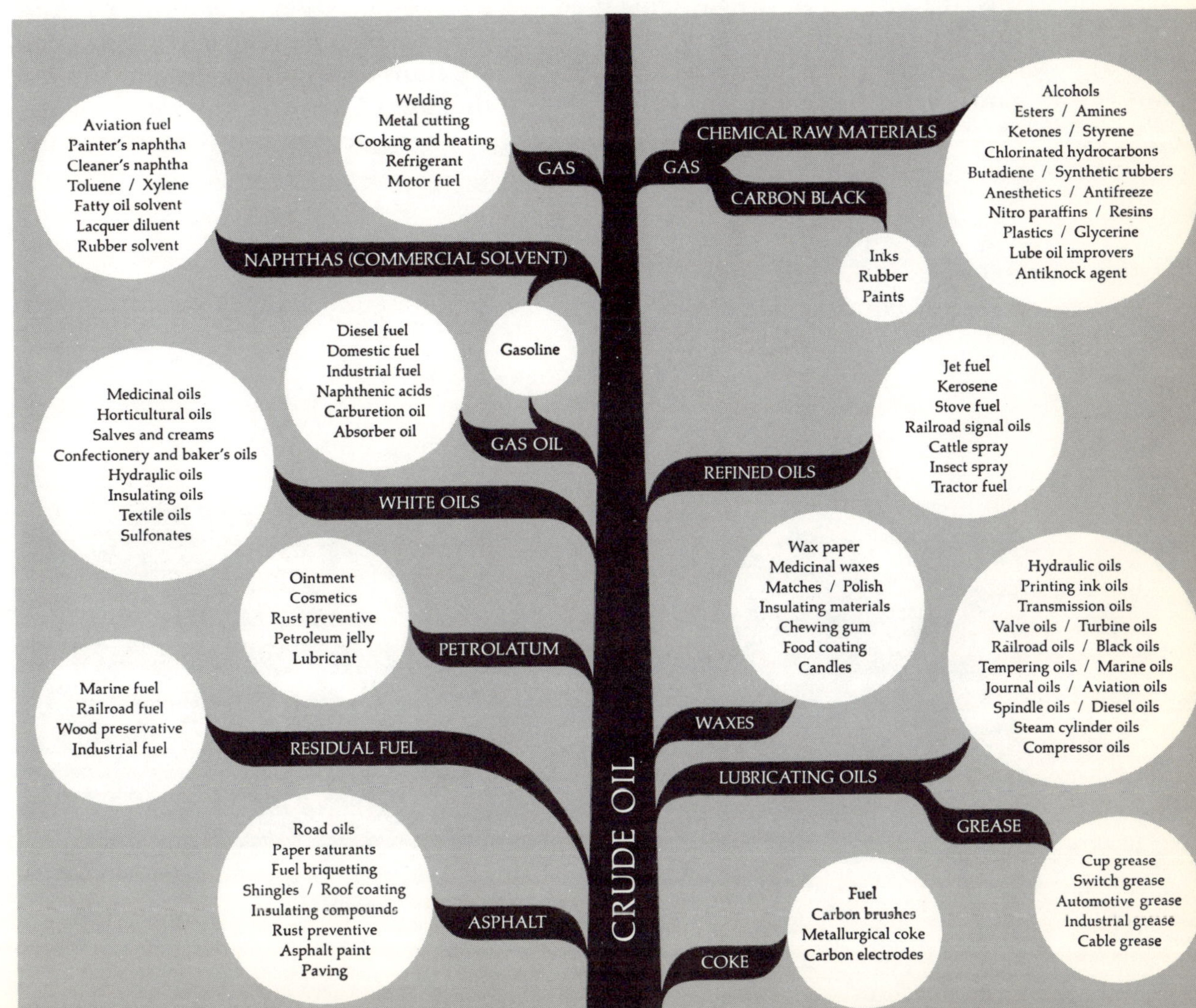

Natural Gas

Natural gas, which is formed by the same processes that produce oil, also usually is discovered with oil. One-third of the natural gas produced in the United States is found in the search for oil. Like coal and oil, natural gas has been known for a long time. At least 2,000 years ago the Chinese piped it through bamboo reeds and burned it as fuel. But it is only in the last century that its use as a fuel has come into its own. Strangely enough, the way was prepared for it by manufactured gas, the gas that is still used for cooking and heating in most cities.

Manufactured gas is made from coal or oil (or even natural gas). It was first burned in the gaslights used in England in the 18th century. The first gas company in America was organized in Baltimore in 1816. By 1858, there were 297 American companies, all producing manufactured gas, and only one producing natural gas. This was located in Fredonia, New York where a reservoir of natural gas had been discovered in 1821.

Natural gas is more efficient than manufactured gas because it gives about twice as much heat; both are smokeless and ashless. The main component of natural gas is methane, a compound of carbon and hydrogen. Natural gas with a high sulfur content smells "sour," otherwise it is practically odorless. In the West, natural gas is less costly than manufactured gas because most gas fields are in that area and in the Southwest. Consumers in the East must pay for its transportation from western fields.

It was mainly the lack of appropriate transportation means that limited the use of natural gas for so many years. The gas must be forced by

Pipes transport gas over large distances.

A pumping station relays the gas onward.

pressure from its storage place, often below ground in depleted oil fields, through the pipelines to its destination. Large, strong pipe was not available for long-distance distribution until a 1,000 mile gas-pipeline was completed in 1931. Today, there are about 750,000 miles of pipeline criss-crossing the nation.

Natural gas is used for cooking, heating, refrigeration, air-conditioning, laundering, and incineration. About 75 per cent of all natural gas, however, is used as a fuel by industry to generate power or heat. In 1920, natural gas accounted for less than 5 per cent of the energy used in the United States; coal supplied 78 per cent, oil 13 per cent, and water power 4 per cent. Today, natural gas supplies 30 per cent of our energy; coal supplies 23 per cent, oil 43 per cent, and water power still 4 per cent.

Like oil, natural gas also yields many important products. It is used in the production of synthetic fabrics and rubbers, ammonia and other chemicals, paints, fertilizer, insecticides, and plastics. "Natural gasoline" and other natural gas liquids are extracted from natural gas. Natural gas is an important component of motor and aviation gasolines. Liquefied petroleum gas is the bottled gas seen in bright-colored containers at suburban and rural homes. It is obtained from the combination of natural crude oil and gas as they come to the surface in oil or gas wells. Inside the tank the gas is actually a liquid; when released, it becomes a gas.

Since natural gas is so closely associated with oil, that is, it is formed, found and extracted under similar conditions, it requires similar conservation methods.

Iron And Steel

The Iron Age dates back to the time when man learned to smelt or separate iron from its ores by heat and hammer it into tools and weapons. Historians estimate that time to be around 1200 B. C., although iron beads and a sickle dating back to 4000 B. C. have been found in Egyptian tombs. The Hittites, a warlike people of Asia Minor, probably were the first to smelt iron on a large scale. Their ability to forge weapons and tools was the source of their power. For two centuries iron-making was their secret; then they were conquered and their knowledge of making iron was spread through the ancient world.

Today, iron and steel (which is a refined and a stronger form of iron) are the basis of our industrial economy. Many of our most important products are made from it and almost everything else is produced or processed by machinery made from iron or steel.

Iron ore, one of the most common of all minerals, makes up about one-fifth of the earth's land surface. Not all of the ore, however, contains enough iron or is in the right place for mining and shipping. Good iron ores, such as brick-red hematite and black magnetite, contain about 52 per cent iron, combined with smaller percentages of other minerals. So great is the demand for iron that even low-grade ore has become one of the most important sources. Taconite, for example, an abundant but very low grade ore, is used today because scientists have found a way to reduce it to iron-rich pellets.

To obtain pure iron, the oxygen and other impurities must be removed from the ore. For thousands of years this was done by smelting it over charcoal. In fact, some European forests were seriously depleted because so much wood was cut for charcoal. The charcoal, however, did not create temperatures high enough for smelting and the impure iron (slag) had to be smelted several times before it was malleable enough to be hammered into shape.

Coal was then tried for smelting. It created the necessary temperature but added sulfur and the phosphorous impurities to the iron. The fuel used today is coke, a "baked" soft coal; it produces the required heat without the impurities.

Iron ore, coke, and limestone are placed into huge blast furnaces and heated to temperatures of 3,000°F. For every ton of iron, the blast furnace produces about six tons of gas and half a ton of slag. The gas is drawn off and used as fuel and the slag is used to make concrete. The molten iron that is produced is pig iron. Pig iron is rigid and will support heavy weights, but it is brittle. When pig iron is cast into molds, it is known as cast iron. Most automobile blocks, for example, are made of cast iron. Most pig iron is refined further into steel by great open-hearth or electric furnaces.

As much as half of the iron used to make steel is scrap iron that has been melted down. This is good conservation practice and good economics because it re-uses materials in a new form. Substitute materials for iron and steel will further reduce the demand for ores as, for example, the use of strong, rigid plastics or light metals for auto or plane bodies. The search goes on for newer and better methods of producing iron and steel, as in using low-grade ores like taconite.

Strip-mining of iron ore, however, is undesirable because the land that is exploited destroys the balance of nature and blights the landscape.

Bethlehem Steel

Piles of iron ore waiting to be sent to the blast furnaces.

A rolling mill. Inland Steel Co.

A blast furnace. Aikins

Strip steel. Carnegie-Illinois Steel

Other Metals

Long before he used iron, man used other metals. He shaped his first metal tools and weapons from pure copper nuggets. Gold and silver, which also are found in the pure state, served as ornaments. Later he learned to mix tin and copper to produce bronze, an alloy which was harder than either of the metals alone. Although iron is harder than bronze, man continued to use bronze well into the Iron Age because it was easier to shape and more reliable than early, brittle forms of iron.

The American Indian mined solid copper in upper Michigan long before Columbus arrived in the New World. Today, copper is extracted from chalcopyrite, cuprite, bornite and other copper-bearing ores. There are large deposits in Michigan, Montana, Tennessee, and Utah, as well as in Australia, Chile, Peru, Africa, and Japan. Copper remains one of the most important metals, but for a different reason. It is a good conductor of electricity.

Aluminium Corp.

Mining bauxite for aluminum.

Aluminum, another very important metal in today's world, has strength, lightness, and resistance to rust. It is extracted mainly from bauxite, an abundant mineral that is a compound of aluminum, oxygen, and water. Pure bauxite is slightly gray but the iron in it turns it red or brown. Bauxite forms from the weathering of aluminum-containing rocks. The main deposit in the United States is in Arkansas, but it is also mined in Alabama, Georgia, and Tennessee. Corundum (from which we get rubies and sapphires), cryolite, and byonite are other aluminum-bearing minerals.

Aluminum is usually regarded as the lightest metal, but magnesium is about one-third lighter. Unlike aluminum, pure magnesium burns; but in combination with copper and

Brown Photos

Strip mining of copper ore.

other metals, it is a fireproof alloy of great strength. Magnesium is extracted from salt water and salt deposits, and it is also made from the mineral, magnesite.

Titanium is another light metal, twice as heavy as magnesium but weighing only half as much as steel. Titanium is used in steel alloys, cutting tools, and paints. Because of its high melting point, it is a strategic metal used in the construction of rockets and supersonic jet planes. Abundant deposits of titanium ores — rutile and ilmenite — are found in Virginia, Florida, Quebec, northern New York, and North Carolina.

Other important metals are: manganese, chromite, tungsten, molybdenum and vanadium, all of which add strength and hardness to steel in alloys; nickel, which in alloys makes metals stronger and corrosion-resistant; lead, which is used in gasoline, batteries, pigment, and chemicals; zinc, used in galvanized steel; platinum, which is resistant to corrosion and has a high melting point;

and tin, the only non-toxic industrial metal.

Some metals are very rare. Platinum, for example, is 100 times rarer than gold. Others, such as gold and manganese, are rare in the United States but plentiful in other lands. Tin is not found at all in our country. The United States has an abundance of most metals, although some have been mined extensively. It is estimated that we have mined 80 per cent of the known lead reserves in the nation, 60 per cent of the known copper reserves, and 80 per cent of the known silver reserves.

Fortunately, new deposits of these metals are constantly being discovered, and scientists continue to seek substitutes for the rarer metals. As in the case of iron, scrap metals of all kinds are now recovered and reprocessed. Scrap aluminum and copper have become a major source for those metals and scrap lead accounts for more than half of the source of lead produced. This is good conservation and good for the economy.

Taconite pellets, a low grade of iron ore.

Titanium will be used on Supersonic Transport Jets.

Prospecting For Minerals

One of the important aspects of mineral conservation, and one that has great possibilities for future geologists and engineers, is the search for new mineral deposits. In the past, these discoveries were made by individual prospectors with a pickax and a knapsack much like the characters seen in television adventure dramas. Today, mineral prospecting is conducted by scientists using electronic devices, photography, chemical analysis, and helicopter.

Sometimes valuable mineral ores are exposed on the surface of the ground. But usually mineral deposits are covered by a mantle of soil and vegetation or hidden deep beneath the rocks. These deposits are uncovered through geochemistry, which combines the methods of geology and chemistry. Since soils are formed largely from rock, the chemical analysis of soil is similar to that of the rocks beneath it. A geochemist can analyze the soil of a region and, if he finds an unusual concentration of traces of a valuable mineral, he suspects a mineral deposit and makes further tests. The same analyses are made of stream sediments which have been washed down from the surrounding land by rain water.

Geochemical prospecting works best in uninhabited or unexplored regions. Where man has settled, geochemists must be careful not to be misled by the traces of civilization. For example, if the average concentration of tin in a stream shows one part per million, then a concentration of ten parts per million would indicate nearby tin deposits. But a discarded tin can lying in the stream bed also would cause a reading of 10 parts per million!

Plants often provide clues to the location of hidden mineral deposits, since they draw their nourishment from elements in the soil. In Colorado, prospectors for uranium and vanadium analyze deep-rooted plants, such as juniper and sage, for traces of these minerals. In Zambia, prospectors for copper look for the "copper flower" which grows only on soils with a high copper content. In Poland, zinc prospectors look for the calamine violet found only in zinc-rich soils.

With modern electronic equipment, prospectors can pinpoint mineral deposits from the air. Two helicopters fly over an area at constant speeds, one about 1,000 feet behind the other. The second helicopter directs electromagnetic waves at the ground, which bounce off and are picked up by delicate instruments on the first aircraft. Since the deflection of the electromagnetic waves varies, depending on the minerals in the rocks below, the presence of mineral deposits will show up in the readings on the leading helicopter's instruments.

Oceanographers tell us that great mineral wealth lies on the deep sea floor in the form of manganese, cobalt, copper, and nickel enclosed in black nodules; that in shallow water off Southern California are millions of tons of phosphates; that off Florida, India, Japan, Australia are iron ores. Prospecting points the way, but the problems involved in drilling, mining, and using the ores are still to be solved.

The striped pole counts silver atoms, if present.

A neutron generator and instruments are stationed 150 feet away.

U.S. Geological Survey

U.S. Dept. of Interior

Helium

Continuous research, both basic and applied, is the key to the conservation of any natural resource. It is particularly important in the conservation of minerals, since they cannot be replaced once they are depleted.

Mineral conservation depends upon greater efficiency in exploring and mining, less waste in the extracting and refining processes, and planning reserves for future use. A great deal has been accomplished by research in laboratories. For example, there are new uses for mica which had previously been lost in processing, and the phosphoric acid industry in Idaho salvages marketable products from materials that had once been discarded.

One of the greatest accomplishments in minerals research has been the conservation of helium under the program of the Bureau of Mines, the Department of the Interior, and industry. The conservation program saves helium that had previously been wasted at the rate of 275 million cubic feet each month. Helium supplies were once expected to last only until about 1985; now reserves are expected to last well beyond the year 2000.

Helium once was known as a safe, nonflammable gas for lifting blimps and dirigibles into the air. But, since 1950, helium has been used in many additional ways. It protects metals from contamination during arc-welding; it tests vital parts of missiles for leaks; it is used in rockets. Helium is also used in components of air-conditioners and refrigerators. It is being tested as a control for quality in hundreds of items — from wines to wonder drugs. It provides the power with which rocket engines eject liquid fuels, and it also seems to be a conductor for heat from nuclear furnaces.

NASA

A tank of helium on Surveyor helps set it down gently 246,000 miles away.

In research dealing with low temperatures, helium is indispensable since it is the only substance on earth through which scientists can come within less than one degree of reaching the absolute zero mark of -459.72°F. Helium also promises to speed the tapping of the wealth of the oceans by helping to prevent absorption of nitrogen into the human bloodstream. With helium,

Privately-owned helium plant produces helium for government use.

men will be able to live and work under tons of water almost as comfortably as they do on dry land.

The new uses for helium and the many additional ores yet to be discovered draw heavily upon our resources. The United States alone is expected to need two billion cubic feet of helium annually by the year 2000, an increase of more than a billion cubic feet.

All known helium resources are in a few natural gas fields in southwestern United States. Previously, when the gas was burned, helium rose to the atmosphere as a waste. Under the Helium Act, the federal government — through the Bureau of Mines — buys the helium. As a result, commercial producers have built and operated five plants to extract helium from the natural gases, three in Kansas and two in Texas. The helium is sold to the government, transported by pipeline to a depleted natural gas field near Amarillo, Texas, and stored for future use.

Research and conservation have thus helped to uncover new uses for an important mineral, and have made possible the production of great quantities that otherwise would have been wasted.

USDA

Scientific farming. In one operation the farmer plows, plants seed, sprays against insects and weeds and fertilizes. No longer does he have to go out time after time to cultivate his crop.

NASA

CHAPTER 8

LOOKING TO THE FUTURE

Although man has been using the materials of the environment for thousands of years, never before have so many people benefited from these materials. Millions of people are engaged in logging, mining, farming, shipping, refining, manufacturing, and selling products made from natural resources to meet an almost limitless demand. During the last twenty years products have been introduced that would have seemed "wild" a generation earlier and old products are in greater demand than ever before.

Eighty million automobiles on the highways mean a great demand for steel, gasoline, rubber, and a hundred other items made from wood, oil, or metal. The increased use of washing machines, dryers, and other household appliances calls for additional supplies of steel, water, electricity. Millions of passengers traveling by jet planes and diesel-powered trains and ships, together with an active demand for military transport mean a greater demand for minerals and fuels. New types of metals and fuels must be found that will withstand the intense heat and speed of rocket propulsion. The explosion of knowledge has caused a parallel explosion in the demand for books printed on paper. Huge power plants, each consuming vast supplies of coal and waterpower, must keep pace with the demand for electricity. Greater use of heavy machinery on farms and in factories calls for more metal, more lubricants.

Can we meet these demands indefinitely or will they be too great a strain on available supplies? Happily, the outlook is a good one — if wise management is practiced. For example, greater efficiency in mining and refining resources reduces waste and, in some instances, waste products are put to new uses. New chemical combinations found in laboratory research improve the quality of wood, steel, paper, and oil or create substitutes in the form of plastics. New products mean new industries and continued prosperity.

The unending curiosity and resourcefulness of the human mind, coupled with the needs of the time, promise still further developments — and, perhaps further complications. Scientists are seeking sources of energy other than water and fossil fuels, energy from the tides, the sun, or atomic fission. They are probing the ocean's depths for new sources of minerals, food, and water.

With access to the seas on an equal basis, poorer nations will be able to get new sources of materials. With solar or atomic energy, nations with limited natural resources will no longer depend on other nations who control crude oil or coal supplies. In short, in this interdependent world, natural resources need to be distributed to improve the living standards of people everywhere.

Meeting The Needs Of Technology

Synthetic proteins from hydrocarbons were used to make the bread.

The United States has an abundance of oil resources. It produces more than two and a half billion barrels of crude oil in a single year, from which a long list of products emerge — oils to run cars, planes, trucks, trains and ships; oils for heating homes and factories, for asphalt and lubricants; products made from chemicals taken from petroleum in the refining processes. Petrochemicals, as these substances are called, are used to make synthetic fabrics of nylon, orlon, and dacron. They are used in the production of fertilizers, insecticides, perfumes, synthetic rubber, and floor waxes. Petrochemical combinations yielded a synthetic protein used to enrich bread products.

The plastics industry, vast creation of the petrochemical field, has found ways of bypassing, improving, or reusing natural substances such as wood, ores, or plant fibers. There are alkyd molding compounds used for electrical accessories; melamine for lighting fixtures; thermoplastics for gears, hinges, and tracks; polyethylene and urethane for pipes, electrical insulation and many, many more items. Countries with limited supplies of minerals and oil are better able to be self-sustaining by producing important items of plastic.

Yet, in spite of our great resources, the demand for oil continues to mount and new sources of supply must be found. Space probes need huge amounts of propellants. A single Saturn missile, for example, uses 400 tons of propellants during the first stage of firing alone; the smaller Atlas missile requires 180 tons per minute. Added to these demands are the military requirement for fuel oil and petrochemicals, and the growth in civilian technology that uses lubricants of all types. Newly-developing nations, too, need oil supplies. New reservoirs of oil are found throughout the world; but the greatest source of supply is probably beneath the ocean.

Allied Chemical

Industrial products are made of plastic.

New kinds of propellants are needed for launching spacecraft.

NASA

Look To The Sea

Semi-submersible drilling rigs.

Just as the 1960's ushered in the Space Age and a worldwide interest in what could be found beyond the earth's atmosphere, the next decade appears to be turning in the direction of "inner space," toward the riches that abound in the seas. This is the last great frontier on earth for finding new natural resources.

Earlier, we learned how sea water along coastal shorelines is beginning to be changed to fresh water. Desalination systems offer great hope for arid lands, especially when the methods are improved and the unit cost is lowered. Power plants using coal or oil for desalination may some day be replaced by atomic reactors.

The ocean abounds in fish, and fishing vessels are tapping the offshore supplies almost without control or regard for the balance of nature, except for an international treaty limiting the take of whales and seals.

Geologists believe that hundreds of billions of barrels of oil can be tapped from beneath the ocean floor; and where there is oil there is usually natural gas. More than 180 drilling rigs are probing the continental shelves of sixty countries in the worldwide hunt for oil. Some rigs stand on giant legs as high as 350 feet, supporting a platform with an area of almost half an acre. A type of rig that is growing in importance is the floating rig. Some are ships equipped with elaborate drilling equipment; others are semi-submersible.

The greatest supply of riches is in the mineral deposits below the seas. Diamonds, cobalt, manganese, titanium, iron ore, copper, and many other valuable substances are there, only to be drilled. The Russians are scouring the floor of the Pacific Ocean for manganese. The United States Bureau of Mines uses underwater television, electronic soundings, and complicated drills at its oceanographic research station in California to explore the sea depths for minerals.

The question arises: to whom do offshore ocean depths belong? The exploration and mining of the seas may touch off a competition among nations that would be much more serious than the race for a new route to India in the 16th century, and as serious as the race for the control of outer space. The possibility for making use of the untapped wealth under the seas lies in international agreements. For example, the Antarctic Treaty of 1960 brought all scientific explorations and discoveries into international jurisdiction. It was signed by t w e l v e nations, including the United States and the Soviet Union. The Treaty requires that the Antarctic be used only for scientific research and for peaceful purposes.

The oceans, too, can be put under international control. A practical solution may be the creation of a United Nations Marine Resources Agency, recommended by the Commission to Study the Organization of Peace. The Agency would control all ocean rights and lease or use the resources for the well-being of all nations.

Atomic Energy -- The Impossible Becomes Possible

Philadelphia Electric Co.

Oak Ridge, Tennessee sea water conversion plant.

Oak Ridge Nat. Lab

Model of Long Island nuclear power and desalination plant.

Twenty years ago, when atomic bombs caused huge destruction with accompanying widespread radiation, it was beyond people's imagination to think that the power of the atom would some day be harnessed and controlled for peacetime uses. Even if it were possible on the drawing boards or in the laboratories of the physicists, the cost would be much greater than a single business organization or community could afford.

Yet, by 1966 the atomic industry has come of age and, within another ten or twenty years, its impact will have spread to nations all around the world. Most of the progress has been achieved in nuclear power plants that help to generate electricity. Other developments have been in agriculture and food processing, as well as in biological and medical research.

In 1965, there were twelve civilian atomic reactors producing electricity in ten different states of the United States, with seven more under construction and eight more in planning. The plants were operated and financed by privately-owned and municipal power companies. The Tennessee Valley Authority, pioneer in low-cost electric power, is having an atomic plant built. The cost of producing power with nuclear fusion has become low enough to meet the competition of fossil fuels. The greatest expense remains the cost of building the plants. Atomic reactors are generating electricity in the United Kingdom, France, the Soviet Union, Canada, and the Scandinavian countries.

Atomic plants do not pollute the air with smoke, as do plants that burn coal or oil. They can adjust to sudden changes in demand for power by generating new power very quickly. Such a method would have avoided the great power failure in Northeastern United States in November,

1965. The fear that power plants may be a menace to people living in the area has been allayed with time and experience. Ten years of electric power production at Shippingport, Pennsylvania (the first atomic power plant in the United States), has yielded a perfect safety record. One reason is that great care is taken in designing the atomic core to prevent any form of radiation leak. The other reason is that the amount of uranium used is comparatively small. Where an atomic bomb uses uranium 90 per cent enriched with U-235, the uranium used in an electric power plant is only two to three per cent enriched.

The use of radiation and radio-isotopes promises to help nations conserve soil and produce more food for their growing populations. C r o p losses in the United States each year add up to $12 billion. The Atomic Energy Commission, working with the Department of Agriculture, state agricultural experiment stations, and research institutions have made great strides. The research scientists use radioactive atoms in soil, seeds, or animal foods as "tracers" that can be followed with a geiger counter. From this detective work come better fertilizers and animal diet, and a knowledge of the causes of disease in plants and animals. This type of work uses radioactive isotopes.

Other studies involve the slow application of gamma rays, or radiation, to agricultural products. This destroys insects or bacteria that cause spoilage or inhibits growth between the time a food is picked and the time it is sold. Scientists have found no ill effects to human beings or animals from eating irradiated foods. In fact, health officials in Canada have already approved the irradiation of potatoes.

The International Atomic Energy Association of the United Nations sees great promise in the peaceful uses of atomic energy as a means of closing the gap between the prosperous nations and the underdeveloped countries.

Gamma rays measure effect on plant growth.

The irradiated bags of onions do not sprout and remain clean longer.

Brookhaven Nat. Lab

U of Michigan

Glossary

Atomic Energy, provides a new source of power that does not depend on water, coal, or oil; promotes plant and animal research through radioactive isotopes; improves the quality of fresh vegetables, meats, etc. through irradiation.

Balance of Nature, the state of a natural community in which a certain number of plants are sufficient to provide food and shelter for a certain population of animals. Too many of either would throw off the natural balance. Man is often responsible for destroying the balance.

Condensation, the return of water to the atmosphere by changing it from liquid to gaseous form as it cools.

Conservation, the wise use through proper methods of farming, logging, mining, etc. of available natural resources. It does not imply non-use, but rather wise use.

Desalination, the treatment of sea water to make it useful as fresh water.

Ecology, the science and study of the interrelationships between plants, animals, and the environment.

Erosion, the wearing down of land by the action of wind, rain, and ice. Erosion may be caused by weathering or by improper methods of land use by man.

Evapotranspiration, the loss of water from the evaporation of the water given off by plants.

Forage, the plant supply that serves as food for grazing animals.

Geochemistry, using chemical composition of the soil as a clue in prospecting for minerals.

Hydrocarbons, mineral substances that contain hydrogen and carbon only, used as fuel.

Irrigation, the process by which water is carried from one place to another for the cultivation of crops.

Oceanography, the study of oceans for new sources of natural resources.

Organic Matter, the material of the soil that is made from the decay of living things. Inorganic Matter, the material in the soil that originated as rock, sand, minerals.

Petrochemicals, the products made from crude oil in the refining process.

Pollution, Air, the mixture of chemicals and dust particles with clean air.

Pollution, Water, the contamination of fresh or salt water that affects the ecology of the water environment.

Precipitation, the rain, hail, sleet, dew, snow that falls to the ground and provides moisture.

Predators, animals that prey on other animals as food. They include mountain lions, bears, lions, cougars, and eagles.

Rangeland, that part of land resources that is used for grazing.

Resources, available materials that can be tapped from nature. Renewable resources are soil, plants, trees, wildlife, water. Non-renewable resources are minerals, oil, and open land. Air, sea water and sun are limitless resources.

Silt, the soil carried away by water during heavy rains, snowstorms, or floods and deposited in streams, reservoirs, or on farms.

Smog, a mixture of smoke and fog in polluted air. Smaze, a mixture of smoke and haze. Smust, a mixture of smoke and dust.

Soil Profile, consists of the top soil (most fertile layer), the subsoil, and the weathered rock.

Waste Treatment, the method used in handling waste from industry, farming, homes, etc. An important problem in water pollution.

Watershed, an area of land that holds the source of water in streams, lakes, marshes, rivers, etc.

Windbreak, a planting of bushes or trees on flat farmland to break the force of strong winds; also helps to hold soil and shelter wildlife.

Index